FIRST SCALP FOR CUSTER

William F. "Buffalo Bill" Cody, circa 1876. Cody wore this colorful theatrical outfit at Warbonnet Creek, validating for subsequent stage audiences the attire of a Plains Indian scout.
Courtesy of the Buffalo Bill Historical Center; P.69.30

First Scalp for Custer

The Skirmish at Warbonnet Creek, Nebraska July 17, 1876

with a Short History of the Warbonnet Battlefield

By Paul L. Hedren

Introduction by Don Russell

Revised Edition
Nebraska State Historical Society
Lincoln

Revised Edition, 2005
Printed in the United States of America

FIrst edition 1980 by Arthur H. Clark Company
Bison Book edition 1987 by University of Nebraska Press

Library of Congress Control Number: 2005931553
ISBN 0-933307-30-6
This book is printed on acid-free paper.

Design and layout by Debra Brownson
Maps by Paul L. Hedren and Steve Ryan
Index by Patricia Gaster

Dedicated to William J. Shay
Cavalryman, Park Ranger, Educator, Friend

Contents

Illustrations

Maps

PREFACE

TO THE REVISED EDITION

THE SKIRMISH AT WARBONNET CREEK in remote northwestern Nebraska remains a memorable episode of the Great Sioux War, one of some two-dozen engagements during that prolonged and shattering conflict in 1876 and 1877. At stake in the war was the opening of the luring Black Hills gold fields, the advance of the Northern Pacific Railroad through the Yellowstone River country, and, ultimately, whether the government would ever control the northern tribesmen, most particularly the Lakota or Teton Sioux. The engagement occurred at dawn on July 17, 1876, when Fifth Cavalry troopers commanded by Colonel Wesley Merritt engaged scouts from a Northern Cheyenne village largely belonging to Morning Star (Dull Knife). The Cheyennes were fleeing the Red Cloud Agency, attempting to join kinsmen in the Powder River country. The soldiers were victorious at Warbonnet and the Indians hastily returned to Red Cloud, near Camp Robinson.

Remembered as a timely victory for the army following Custer's horrendous defeat at the Little Big Horn, the Warbonnet skirmish featured one memorable act, Buffalo Bill Cody's killing and scalping of a Cheyenne warrior later identified as Yellow Hair. As troopers rode by during the unfolding action, Cody lofted Yellow Hair's scalp and proclaimed it the "first scalp for Custer," which it probably was.

This episode, and a good deal more, is the story told in *First Scalp for Custer: The Skirmish at Warbonnet Creek, Nebraska, July 17, 1876*. First published by the Arthur H. Clark Company in 1980 and reprinted by the University of Nebraska Press in 1987, copies of this slender history have long been generally unavailable; when found, a Clark first edition commands hundreds of dollars.

To the author's pleasure, demand for the book persists, and it continues to be cited by scholars recounting the fascinating saga of the Great Sioux War. It has not been supplanted.

This revised edition by the Nebraska State Historical Society expands the Warbonnet story considerably by adding details unavailable when the account was composed in the late 1970s, by more broadly developing Cody's actions in the skirmish, by offering a more relevant introduction to and assessment of the engagement, by adding a number of different illustrations, and by updating the history of the site, which remains exceedingly remote and fortunately well preserved.

Paul L. Hedren
O'Neill, Nebraska
January 2005

Acknowledgments

MANY INDIVIDUALS AND INSTITUTIONS assisted in the preparation of this study of the skirmish at Warbonnet Creek, then and now. In the late 1970s Dale E. Floyd, National Archives; John J. Slonaker, U. S. Army Military History Research Collection; Cassandra Tiberio, University of Colorado Libraries; Richard I. Frost, Buffalo Bill Historical Center; Harry H. Anderson, Milwaukee County Historical Society; Marie T. Capps, U. S. Military Academy Library; Gerald Bardo, Lusk, Wyoming; Jerome A. Greene, Denver; Ann Reinert, Nebraska State Historical Society; B. William and Nadezhda R. Henry, Larned, Kansas; Douglas McChristian, Fort Laramie National Historic Site; Vance E. Nelson, Fort Robinson Museum; and Don Russell, Elmhurst, Illinois, all provided valuable information, encouragement, and counsel.

The result was my first book, which I dedicated to William J. Shay of Torrington, Wyoming. Bill, like Don Russell, personally knew one of the central characters in the story, General Charles King, and one who sought to locate the field in the late 1920s, General William Carey Brown. And Bill was a companion on a memorable visit to the battlefield nearly one hundred years to the day after the fight occurred in 1876, where he and I reveled in our parallel interests in the site and its characters.

I have never shed my enthusiasm for the Warbonnet story and over the years have enjoyed the continued support and encouragement of Eli Paul, Kansas City; Tom Buecker, present curator of the Fort Robinson Museum; Paul Andrew Hutton, Albuquerque; Paul Fees, former senior curator of the Buffalo Bill Historical Center; Steve Friesen, Buffalo Bill Museum and Grave; Brian Dippie, Victoria, British Columbia; Juti Winchester, Lynn Houze, Ann Marie Donoghue, Sarah Boehme, Nathan Bender, and Frances Clymer of today's Buffalo Bill Historical Center; Jim Hatzell, Rapid City; and Jerry Greene,

Denver, all of whom have abetted this interest with glee.

I am especially grateful to Jim Potter and Don Cunningham of the Nebraska State Historical Society, who encouraged this reprint edition and brought tremendous editorial talent to its preparation. And, as always, I acknowledge my girls, Ethne and Whitney, who grew up prowling the Warbonnet field with me, and Connie Burns, who patiently awaits her turn.

To one and all, thank you very much.

A Very Personal Introduction

By Don Russell

MORE THAN HALF A CENTURY AGO I was a member of the editorial staff of *The Chicago Daily News*, a newspaper that has since succumbed to rapidly and inconsistent changes of policy, first marked by one of the least important changes—the dropping of the capitalized "The" from in front of its name. In 1929, however, it was as devoted to literature, science, and the arts as it was to the accuracy and objectivity of its news reporting. It had recently started a mid-week pictorial magazine to offer original short stories and educational features, among which was a column contributed by a staff member, Carl Sandburg. Its editor during most of its brief career was Robert W. Andrews, later of note as writer of radio's "Little Orphan Annie," and still later of scripts for Hollywood.

In one of the early issues, before Andrews took over, there appeared an article purporting to be reminiscences told to the writer by General George Crook. They were so utterly at variance with historical narrative of the campaign of 1876 that I protested, but got nowhere. Later I learned that the writer was a near relative of the editor to whom I had protested. While there was no point in carrying the matter further, for my own satisfaction I wanted to know if I was right. I recalled the title of a book, *Campaigning With Crook*, and found the author's Milwaukee address in *Who's Who in America*. I sent a copy of the article to General Charles King. He replied promptly, agreeing that the story was "fantastic." He asked that he not be quoted, insisting that he should not be drawn into controversy.

With the passing of years, I have become tolerant of such fantastic yarns. When you try to recall events of half a century ago, as I am doing now, you are in trouble. When you try to recall what someone told you decades ago, you are in deep trouble. Some useful facts may be gleaned from narratives garbled by faulty memory. Happily the out-and-out liars are fewer, although the Indian wars seem to have spewed out an inordinate amount of prevarication. The motives would seem to be self-aggrandizement and jealousy of those receiving credit or popular acclaim.

I expressed my appreciation to General King and considered the matter closed, but only two days later I received a four-page letter from him, written in his small but legible script, in which I learned that King had already been drawn into controversy, which he apparently assumed had occasioned my inquiry. The controversy concerned a book, *The Making of Buffalo Bill*, by Richard J. Walsh in collaboration with Milton S. Salsbury. This was a period when debunking biography was highly popular and the late William F. Cody was obviously a likely subject. The title implied that Buffalo Bill had been "made" by press agentry, and it must be admitted that Cody had done little to restrain the extravagances of his show's publicity staff. To his credit the author had sought source material, some of it of considerable value. However, he had also used uncritically some of the fantasies of faulty memory, as well as some provable out-and-out lies. Such products casting doubt on Cody's achievement in the fight on the Warbonnet incensed King, who not only had witnessed the incident but who had taken a prominent part in the action. At issue was the killing of an Indian called Yellow Hand, or Hay-o-wei, more accurately translated, said King, as Yellow Hair because of a scalp he wore.

King's letter to me told this story in detail, although he referred me to his account in *Campaigning With Crook*, originally written only four years after the fight. He also recalled that at Cody's request he had written a description of the fight for the *New York Herald* when the troops reached Fort Laramie July 21, four days after the action, but he had never seen his piece in print. On my expressing interest in the problem, King offered to stop by and see me on his next trip to Chicago, the occasion being, I believe, a dinner of West Point alumni.

He arrived late in the afternoon. My desk, reputedly once used by Eugene Field, was in a triangular area fenced off to the right of a creaking slow elevator in a conglomeration of old buildings at various levels that recalls an observance of one of my elder colleagues: "How Dickens would have reveled in this place." Everyone in the immediate area had gone home except Mrs. Maude Robinson, a writer of newspaper fiction, who, on learning that King was coming, had begged to be allowed to stay on the promise of keeping quiet and busy. She had read King's books. Our office was not well lighted, and I recall him as a somewhat shadowy figure.

Without much preliminary, as I recall, he told the story of the Warbonnet fight as he had witnessed it. It was not an event of vast historic importance, but it had the elements that make the early West seem romantic; the substance of the Western in fiction, fact, and drama exploited in novel, movie, radio, and television, all of which together cannot have the impact of one who tells it as it was because he was there. However, his memory was reaching back half a century, and another half century has passed since that story was told. I will not try to reconstruct it, although I find some notes apparently taken at the time. The most accuracy can be expected in the version recorded closest to the time of the action.

Research is often frustrating. A file of the *New York Herald* for 1876 was found in a Chicago library, but the issue of July 23 was missing. The article sought was located and copied from a file in the library of the University of Michigan. Apparently whatever King had written had been incorporated in a lengthy article covering the campaign. King repudiated it. It was not at all as he remembered it.

The story as King told it to me seemed at the time to be not very different from what he had written in the letter. The letter is close to what he wrote in *Campaigning With Crook*. The wording differed, but there were characteristic phrasings. Some of those phrasings occurred in the *New York Herald* article. It probably was printed as King wrote it, with possibly slight changes to fit it into a running story.

Other participants were available. Frederick Post, retired sergeant of Company C, wrote to General King recalling the names of the two couriers whose rescue was the object of Cody's exploit. The names were verified in the regiment's muster rolls. Another eyewitness who proved to be much interested was Chris Madsen, a signalman stationed on a butte not far from the scene of action. Cody, returning from his early morning scouting, stopped by Madsen's post and asked him to signal that the Indians were moving out, then rode on to report added details. Madsen, a recent immigrant from Denmark, was a veteran of the Danish-Prussian and Franco-Prussian wars and had served with the French Foreign Legion in Algeria. In later years he became famous as a frontier peace officer in Oklahoma's "No Man's Land," associated with Bill Tilghman and Heck Thomas.

King and Madsen journeyed to western Nebraska to pick sites for monuments planned by the Nebraska State Historical Society. (They were dedicated in 1934.) King expressed doubt that the exact spot had been located. Madsen was confident it had. Madsen also disagreed on many details of King's story, listing twenty-six items in five pages of comments on *Campaigning With Crook,* and placed copies "not for publication" with historical societies. Some were of minor importance, but Madsen had doubts about the couriers, and the wagon train, and was emphatic that there was no infantry with the wagon train. King had sought Merritt's report of the fight in War Department records—this was before the days of the National Archives—and not finding it after considerable help by those in charge, concluded that because of the pressures of the campaign, Merritt had overlooked writing one. Some years later I called for Merritt's report at the National Archives and got it. It agreed with King on the infantry, the wagon train, and the couriers. By another bit of serendipity, Mrs. Minnie D. Millbrook told me of seeing something about Buffalo Bill in the 1876 file of the *Ellis County Star.* This was run down with the aid of Nyle H. Miller and the Kansas State Historical Society and proved to be an article written at the time by Sergeant John Powers, who saw the Warbonnet fight from the wagon train, again confirming King's story.

Thus the story of a minor fight is built up. The nearer the writing is to the action, the more accurate the result will be, but witnesses will rarely agree on all details. A sufficient weight of eyewitness evidence discredits the fantastic yarns, of which an excessive number have accumulated around Cody's exploits.

The result of our association was an article, "My Friend, Buffalo Bill," as told by General Charles King to Don Russell, published in *The Cavalry Journal* of September-October 1932. We collaborated on another article for the same publication, and he formed the habit of stopping by whenever he came to Chicago, commonly once a month. Some portraits used in his books give the impression of a large, almost portly, person; actually he was very small, barely over the army's height requirement, and when I knew him, very lean, with skin tightly drawn and ruddy, but he was alert and active, dashing along at a military pace, very erect, and swinging a cane. Although quick mentally and in speech, he distrusted his memory and on occasion, when asked a question, deferred the answer until "next time," after he had thought the subject through. He never failed to remember "next time." In this period he rode horseback as grand marshal of Milwaukee's Memorial Day parade, he inspected the cadets at St. John's Military Academy, and he continued his longtime association with the Wisconsin National Guard. An official document credited him with seventy years of active service.

During a trip to Washington he was given a physical examination and army doctors told him he seemed good for ten years yet—"and I can use every minute of it," he said intently. He did not make the ten years, but he made use of every minute until his death March 17, 1933, at the age of eighty-eight years, five months, and five days. King had his faults; serious ones, yet to be viewed with considerable tolerance; for without them, by a curious paradox, he might have missed some of his outstanding accomplishments. Despite reversals, he kept up the good fight and never stopped trying. For this he has my admiration. It seems fitting to pass on his torch to Paul L. Hedren for his retelling in a new guise of the eventful campaign of the Fifth Regiment of United States Cavalry in the days of Charles King.

Chapter 1

To Warbonnet

By LATE JUNE 1876 the U.S. Army's notion of a quick hitting, wintertime campaign against nonreservation Sioux Indians had been foiled, and badly. Patterned in orchestration after the recently successful Red River War against Comanche, Kiowa, and Southern Cheyenne Indians in Texas and Indian Territory, independent columns of soldiers invaded eastern Montana and northern Wyoming seeking the northern roamers, as the unyielding Sioux were often called. On the Powder River in southeastern Montana on March 17 the first of the columns struck an Indian village containing some one hundred lodges. The fighting lasted most of the day before the soldiers unceremoniously withdrew, thinking, however, that they had bested a camp belonging to Crazy Horse. Instead, the Indians were Northern Cheyennes led by Old Bear, and the action brought those steadfast friends of the Sioux into the war. Three months later, and again in southeastern Montana, soldiers and tribesmen clashed, first on Rosebud Creek on June 17, and then calamitously on the Little Big Horn River on June 25. In both instances, the soldier columns reeled.

While most of the early fighting of the Great Sioux War occurred across a sweeping and desolate Montana landscape on what soon came to be considered the "war front," or northern front, this dramatic conflict with the Sioux had a vigorously contested southern front as well. The countryside lying between the Union Pacific Railroad in Nebraska and Wyoming northward to the Black Hills gold fields in Dakota witnessed its own incessant turmoil as thousands of "Hillers" trekked to the new El Dorado on undefended roads, passing en route a bandit- and Indian-infested no man's land north of Fort Laramie, plus the treacherous Powder River Trail connecting the Red Cloud and Spotted Tail agencies and the warring camps and, on the Sidney Road, the very proximity of those sizeable Nebraska agencies. Of the two main roads north, via Sidney, Nebraska, and Cheyenne, Wyoming, clearly the latter was preferred. The Cheyenne route approached the Black Hills from the southwest and initially availed itself of military protection at venerable Fort Laramie, albeit limited, and the army's newly completed iron truss bridge nearby that spanned the ever-turbulent North Platte River. The road itself was not shielded from Indians or road agents, however, and during the winter and spring of 1876 Cheyenne's partisans beseeched the army for protection.

In Chicago, Lieutenant General Philip H. Sheridan, commanding the vast Military Division of the Missouri, encompassing in its northern realm the entire Sioux War zone, had many reasons to appease Wyoming's citizens. Certainly, safeguarding the Black Hills gold fields and their access routes had economic consequences benefiting the nation. Important, too, troops deployed across the southern margins of the war zone might well shape the outcome on the northern front by stemming the unfettered passage of fighting men and materiel from the Nebraska agencies that served to embolden already headstrong leaders, such as Crazy Horse and Sitting Bull.

With fortunate calm in most other sectors of his administrative division, Sheridan readily mobilized additional troops for service in the Great Sioux War as demands arose. Among the first called forth, in what in the long run amounted to a sweeping redeployment of the army to fight the Sioux, was the Fifth Cavalry Regiment, then generally scattered at posts along the Kansas Pacific Railroad and in the Indian Territory in the Military Department of the Missouri. Commanded in the field by its lieutenant colonel, Eugene A. Carr, and soon by Colonel Wesley Merritt, a renowned Civil War cavalry commander, the "Dandy Fifth" was a superb outfit with a distinctive élan and considerable experience in Indian warfare. Initially, eight companies were detailed for duty in Wyoming and Nebraska. Even the regiment's old friend from earlier days on the central Plains, William F. "Buffalo Bill" Cody, quickly joined the expedition. Within weeks of receiving orders, the Fifth was positioned at the intersection of the Indians' Powder River Trail and Cheyenne-Black Hills Road, and from near that perch on July 17 gained the honor of striking at Warbonnet Creek, Nebraska, the first appreciable victory for the United States Army in the Great Sioux War.[1]

News emanating from the northern Plains in early 1876 was ominous, and the muster of the Fifth Cavalry for service in the Military Department of the Platte was not entirely unexpected by the headquarters detachment and resident companies at Fort Hays, Kansas, or another company recently arrived from Fort Riley and momentarily residing in tents along the Smoky Hill River. Confirming orders dispatching eight companies to the Sioux War came in late May, and Lieutenant Colonel Carr had Hays's residents and tented guests hurriedly en route by rail to Denver and Cheyenne. In turn, orders received in Cheyenne soon had the regiment bounding north to Fort Laramie. Laramie was a strategically located staging area at a pivotal intersection where traffic, availing itself of the new North Platte River bridge, turned northwestward to Fort Fetterman, maintained a northerly course to the Black Hills, or headed northeastward to Camps Robinson and Sheridan and the Red Cloud and Spotted Tail Indian agencies.[2]

The Fifth Cavalry's camp at Fort Laramie covered a large expanse about a mile east of the post, near the confluence of the North Platte and Laramie rivers. Sheridan had designated Fort Laramie as the Fifth's official supply depot and the cavalrymen busily drew supplies from commissary and quartermaster storehouses. Post trader John S. Collins did a thriving business as well at his store, troopers purchasing last minute stocks of tobacco, canned goods, floppy-brimmed hats, and other personal items before embarking for the field. Some of the Fifth's officers found time to socialize with members of the garrison, but preparing for the new campaign was the overriding concern. On June 20 two more companies arrived and went into camp alongside their comrades.[3]

While at Fort Laramie, Carr, commanding the regiment, received orders from Sheridan outlining the role his cavalry would play in the ensuing weeks. "The Lieutenant General Commanding," the orders read,

> directs you to proceed, with 8 companies of the Fifth Cavalry, on the road from Fort Laramie to Custer City until you reach the crossing of the main Powder River trail leading from the vicinity of Red Cloud Agency westward to Powder and Yellowstone Rivers. Arriving at that point, you will follow the trail westward, proceeding such distances as your judgment and the amount of supplies which you carry will warrant.[4]

In the eyes of many, the order to commence a new movement on the southern front came none too soon. Persistent rumors of Indian bands leaving the Red Cloud and Spotted Tail agencies in Nebraska troubled local residents and Black Hills-bound "Hillers" alike, and bloodshed on the roads was pitifully common. Perhaps the Fifth would help stem the tide. Before Carr departed, several jurisdictional and personnel matters were set straight. In mid-June, a subunit of the Department of the Platte, the District of the Black Hills, was reestablished with Carr as its commander. This district embraced parts of western Nebraska and Dakota along with eastern Wyoming to, but not including, Fort Fetterman on the North Platte River northwest of Fort Laramie. As commander, Carr was responsible for protecting white settlers within the district.[5] Serving as Carr's chief administrative aide, First Lieutenant William C. Forbush, then the Fifth's adjutant, was named acting assistant adjutant general for the District of the Black Hills. In Forbush's stead, First Lieutenant Charles King was advanced to acting adjutant of the regiment. King, a thirty-two-year-old West Point graduate and veteran of Apache campaigning in Arizona several years earlier, was an able soldier and gifted writer. In all, he penned some half a dozen different accounts of the regiment's participation in the Sioux War and emerged as one of the conflict's chief chroniclers.[6]

William F. "Buffalo Bill" Cody served as the Fifth's chief of scouts. When Cody learned that his favorite regiment was bound for the field, he abandoned the Eastern stage and sought out its camp. Cody's abilities as an Indian scout and plainsman were well known and appreciated, and Carr had even written Sheridan to learn of his whereabouts. Upon Cody's arrival, Private Daniel Brown of the headquarters detachment recorded:

> All the old boys in the regiment upon seeing General Carr and Cody together, exchanged confidences, and expressed themselves to the effect that with such a leader and scout they could get away with all the Sitting Bulls and Crazy Horses in the Sioux tribe.[7]

Cody, at age thirty, indeed enjoyed fame beyond his years. While in his teens he had signed on as a Pony Express messenger. He later served with Kansas troops during the Civil War and subsequently engaged as a buffalo hunter in 1867–68, supplying meat to construction workers advancing the Kansas Pacific Railroad, where he rightly earned the name "Buffalo Bill." Cody came to Sheridan's attention after carrying dispatches for the railroad and was offered employment as a scout with the Fifth Cavalry, then serving in Kansas and Nebraska. He figured prominently in Carr's fight with Cheyenne Indians at Summit Springs in 1869, and again as a hunting guide with Sheridan for parties of notables, including in 1872 the Grand Duke Alexis of Russia. These varied, high profile experiences also brought him to the attention of Ned Buntline, a prolific dime novelist, who lured Cody to the stage in 1872, where he delivered crowd pleasing dramatizations of his western adventures.[8]

Cody imparted quite an impression on members of the Fort Laramie garrison as he passed through. "I remember his fine figure," recalled Cynthia Capron, wife of First Lieutenant Thaddeus Capron, Ninth Infantry, "as he stood by the Sutler store, straight and slender, with his scarlet shirt belted in, and his long hair distinguishing him as the well known character so much more widely known since."[9]

On June 20 another scout, Baptiste "Little Bat" Garnier, was directed by Fort Laramie's quartermaster, First Lieutenant Alfred Morton, Ninth Infantry, to report to Carr for duty with the column. Garnier was a professional hunter and interpreter who had lived in the Fort Laramie area since 1868. Earlier in 1876 he served as a scout on the Big Horn Expedition and had participated in the March 17 fight with Northern Cheyenne Indians on the Powder River. The affable and crack-shot Jonathan or Jim White also joined the column. Nick-named "Buffalo Chips," White was Cody's protégé and, according to King, his ever-present "shadow." He had served under Major General J. E. B. Stuart, C.S.A., during the Civil War.[10]

With Cody, Garnier, White, and two additional mixed-blood scouts as-signed at Fort Laramie, the column was thought to be in excellent hands. Cody, however, did not depart with the regiment. Sheridan visited Fort Laramie on June 14, along with aides Colonel James B. Fry and Lieutenant Colonel James W. Forsyth. The party then moved on to inspect Camp Robinson, Nebraska, and the neighboring Indian agencies, with Cody accom-panying. Only later did Buffalo Bill head north.[11]

Carr was apprehensive on the eve of departing Fort Laramie. He wrote his wife:

> I have always been horrified at the idea of killing Indian women and children. I believe I am on record to that effect. If not, it can easily

> be proved that my verbal orders were always that way—that I did not deem it necessary to give written orders, because my command did not require any restraint in that direction. Poor things. I do not blame them for fighting for their husbands and fathers, right or wrong—many white women would do the same.[12]

Carr's attitude, as well as that of many of his fellow officers, may have been shaken by news recently received of Brigadier General George Crook's setback at Rosebud Creek, Montana, on June 17. Crook, with a force of some twelve hundred cavalry and infantry, had been turned away by a smaller number of allied Sioux and Cheyenne Indians. In the eyes of many, that setback made Carr's mission all the more critical.

The regiment broke camp early on June 22, packed last-minute items, and struck across the iron bridge spanning the North Platte, heading northward on the Custer City Road. A contract doctor, Acting Assistant Surgeon Junius W. Powell, with supplies provided from the Fort Laramie hospital, accompanied the force.[13] The column consisted of Companies A, C, D, G, I, K, and M, Fifth Cavalry, plus field and staff, scouts, and headquarters attendants.

Sergeant John Powers of Company A, in a letter to a Kansas newspaper, provided illuminating details on this first day's march.

> We left Fort Laramie on the 22d inst., crossing the North Platte over one of the finest iron bridges I have ever seen west of the Missouri, and then traveled up the east bank of the Platte three miles to Cottonwood creek, up which stream we went eight miles farther. We then struck off over a divide into a small valley for about a mile, where we came to a large water-hole by the side of the road. A few of the boys in their hurry to get water, treated themselves and horses to a cold bath, and one of them received quite serious injuries from his horse by reason of the animal's walking over and pawing him in its effort to get out. About fifteen miles from Fort Laramie we passed the government ranch. The reason of its establishment in such an isolated place is not known to the writer, but it is a strong post, and six or eight men can hold it against as many hundred Indians. After passing by it, we went on thirteen miles further to the south fork of Rawhide creek, where we camped. Water and grass are plenty, but wood was scarce for a large command like this.

Powers's insightful narrative continued:

> On the morning of June 22d [*sic*, the twenty-third] we left camp at half-past 6 a.m., two miles from which we passed the ruins of Rawhide Station, which had been burned by the Indians but ten days before. Our road was through a rough country, covered with sand buttes, prickly pears and sage brush, and too poor for any purposes but grazing. We passed a number of wagon trains coming in from Custer City, during our march.[14]

On the evening of June 23 the command camped at the Cardinal's Chair, a landform near the Niobrara River immediately west of present-day Lusk, Wyoming. On the twenty-fourth the column continued north and before noon had descended into the valley of the Old Woman's Fork of the South Cheyenne River. Around midday dispatches arrived from Fort Laramie. One from Sheridan directed Carr to continue northward on the Custer City Road, but upon reaching the Powder River Trail, he was to halt there and await further instructions.[15]

The dispatch rider returned to Fort Laramie and Carr assembled his officers to plot the next move. Sensing urgency, it was decided that Major Thaddeus Stanton of the Paymaster Department, along on this campaign representing Sheridan's staff, would push ahead with one company, following Indian signs reported by the scouts. The notion was to reach the Powder River Trail as hurriedly as possible in advance of the slower column. Stanton selected for his escort, scout Little Bat Garnier, Lieutenant King, and Company C, commanded by Second Lieutenant Edward Keyes. By 3 P.M. the advance was underway, and within several hours the detachment struck a large and recent Indian trail, "our first . . . of the campaign," recorded King.[16]

Stanton's detail observed Indian campfire smoke at dark and more tracks as they headed on to the Cheyenne, or Mini Pusa, River. By 9 P.M. the command broke the last ridge and descended into the Cheyenne Valley. An hour and a half later they reached the river. After pausing for water, the troopers headed for the northern bluffs and established camp. While Keyes and King posted sentinels, the remainder of the company prepared a hurried meal and then settled in for the night.

At dawn on June 25 the men saddled and, without breakfast, returned to the Cheyenne River, scouring all the while for signs of Indians. Less than half a mile from camp, Little Bat detected hoofprints barely, he thought, two hours old. Confident that they were in no danger, however, the detachment pressed forward.

At about noon Little Bat gestured for Stanton and King to hurry along and then directed their attention to the southeast. With field glasses the officers saw plainly the broad, well-beaten Indian trail. King thought "it looked like a great highway, deserted and silent, and it led from the thick timber in the Cheyenne valley straight to the southeast up the distant slope, and disappeared over the dim, misty range of hills in the direction of the Red Cloud and Spotted Tail reservations."[17]

Stanton secreted his men in the thick cottonwood timber coursing the river bottom and rejoined King on a hilltop, where they could watch for any Indian movement. Behind them they saw dust in the distance, marking Carr's approach. Ahead of them—nothing! The officers groused at their inability to sight Indians. Some three hundred miles away on this very day, along the Little Big Horn River in Montana, George Custer probably grumbled for a moment too.

All the night of June 25 and through the morning of the twenty-sixth, the men maintained a vigil on the Indian trail but never once spotted any activity. At noon Carr rejoined Major Stanton. As the officers interpreted their orders, they were to remain hidden in the broad South Cheyenne River valley and maintain a watch on the Indian trail, putting "an end to the system of reinforcements then in full blast."[18]

Back at Fort Laramie, Company B, Fifth Cavalry, commanded by Captain Robert Montgomery, departed this day for Carr's command. A courier bearing dispatches for the column accompanied "B." Carr, meanwhile, anticipating a need for supplies, requested that an express service be established between Laramie and his command. Apologetically, Major Edwin F. Townsend, Fort Laramie's commander, explained to Carr that he would forward supplies as quickly as possible, but since wagon transportation was in short supply could not dispatch a train until after July 6.[19]

For the next nine days, from June 26 through July 3, the Fifth Cavalry remained encamped along the Cheyenne River. Seventy-five thousand pounds of grain for the cavalry mounts arrived during this period, however, relieving Carr's anxiety, if not an actual shortage.[20] Throughout the span,

Fort Laramie in 1876. An aged but vital post during the long course of the Great Sioux War, Fort Laramie was well positioned on the war's southern front to support troop and supply movements and the feverish Black Hills gold rush.
Courtesy of the National Archives

Lieutenant Colonel Eugene A. Carr. A seasoned field commander, Carr led the Fifth Cavalry during Indian campaigning on the central Plains and in Arizona, but was succeeded at the head of the regiment by Wesley Merritt in mid-1876, to Carr's considerable dismay. Courtesy of the Nebraska State Historical Society; RG2688-PH:11

First Lieutenant Charles King. A gifted storyteller, King penned several critical accounts of the Warbonnet Creek skirmish and the Fifth Cavalry's service during the Great Sioux War, and played a central role in the July 17 action. Courtesy of Paul L. Hedren

▲ North Platte River Bridge at Fort Laramie. Built in 1875 and preserved today by the National Park Service at Fort Laramie National Historic Site, this bridge provided direct passage to the Black Hills gold fields, the Sioux agencies in Nebraska, and the battlefields of the Great Sioux War. Courtesy of Paul L. Hedren

◀ Colonel Wesley Merritt. Merritt assumed command of the Fifth Cavalry on July 1, 1876, and led the regiment at Warbonnet Creek and through the remainder of its eventful participation in the Great Sioux War. Courtesy of the Little Bighorn Battlefield National Monument

companies regularly scouted for Indians, and occasionally small parties of tribesmen were encountered, but pursuit only tired the animals.

The talk of the camp at the end of June was the anticipated change in regimental command. The Fifth's colonel, William H. Emory, was scheduled for retirement at the mandatory age and reports had Lieutenant Colonel Wesley Merritt of the Ninth Cavalry succeeding him. The prospective change met mixed reactions. Emory, an 1831 West Point graduate, had not exercised field command of the Fifth Cavalry for years and any change in that circumstance would be for the better. But not everyone was pleased with the prospect of Merritt taking command, especially Carr, himself an 1850 West Point graduate. Carr, now forty-six, had exercised defacto command of the regiment since 1868 and chafed at the notion of a subordinate role.

Promotion by seniority in grade was a conventional fate in the Regular Army and yet Carr, in a letter to his wife, Mary, confided,

> It is, of course, an humiliation to me to have him come in and take command. It seems curious that the Government should find it necessary to spend large amounts of money and some blood to teach Terry, Crook and Merritt how to fight these Prairie Indians when there are others who know better how to do it.[21]

Privately, Cody, Carr's friend and supporter, expressed a similar sentiment. "I was sorry," he wrote, "that the command was taken from General Carr, because under him it had made its fighting reputation."[22]

Merritt, then forty-two years old, received his promotion effective July 1. Despite Carr's evident contempt and Cody's apprehension, Merritt's assignment to the Fifth Cavalry was propitious. An 1860 West Point graduate, he was among Sheridan's favorite officers, having served throughout the Civil War, including at Gettysburg and thereafter in command of Sheridan's cavalry in the Shenandoah and Appomattox campaigns. In 1866 Merritt was assigned to the newly organized Ninth Cavalry Regiment as its lieutenant colonel and served mostly in Texas. He was detailed as an inspector of cavalry for the Military Division of the Missouri in March 1875, which kept him in Sheridan's eye and brought him to the northern Plains in 1876. Though less seasoned in Indian warfare than Carr, he was a quick study and conducted himself and his new regiment well throughout the Great Sioux War, enjoying a long and meritorious career thereafter.[23]

In another promotion on July 1, Captain Julius W. Mason of Company K was advanced to major, Third Cavalry. Like other senior officers in the regiment, Mason was a respected tactician with many years of exemplary service, including during the Civil War, where he led cavalry troops at Gettysburg and later commanded General Grant's personal escort. When learning of his transfer, however, instead of immediately departing, he chose to prolong his service with the Fifth, even to the conclusion of the current campaign.[24]

Merritt wasted little time joining his new command. At Fort Laramie on June 28, he secured the services of Captain James Egan and Company K, Second Cavalry, Laramie's resident cavalry company that season, to escort him north to the regiment. Personally guiding was Bill Cody, fresh from duty with Sheridan. Merritt reached the cavalry camp on July 1. Early the next morning, in his first exercise of command, he moved the bivouac some four miles closer to the Indian trail. He then detailed Company B to scout eastward toward the Black Hills, and positioned Edward Hayes's Company G on the trail itself. Still, however, no Indians were spotted.[25]

Just after sunup on July 3, as the command was tending its horses and preparing breakfast, Merritt's orderly came rushing through the trees heralding Major Mason. Indians had been sighted within a mile of camp and Merritt wanted Mason's Company K to pursue the interlopers as quickly and aggressively as possible. Within minutes, "K's" horses were saddled and the men mounted and winding their way through cottonwoods and onto the broad, largely dry, streambed of the South Cheyenne.

Apparently a dozen Indians had come to within a mile of the camp before discovering the presence of soldiers. Startled, they turned and fled. Cody was one of the first on their trail, but the Indians had a lead of several miles. Captain Sanford Kellogg's Company I followed "K" within minutes, and soon both outfits were trotting in parallel columns. Though Cody and the scouts on several occasions beckoned the troopers hurriedly over hills as if closing on the Indians, the pursued remained far ahead.

The chase took the cavalrymen in a thirty-mile circle. Occasionally, the troopers encountered pack animals burdened with what King called "fresh agency provisions" abandoned in the flight. And only once did the scouts close the gap sufficiently to warrant exchanging carbine shots. In disgust, at mid-afternoon the companies turned for camp, arriving at 4 P.M., empty-handed and exhausted.[26]

Merritt was confident that the Fifth's presence on the Powder River Trail was known at the agencies and he determined to move to the army stockade guarding Sage Creek. Intent at the same time on maintaining vigilance, he divided the regiment into three battalions. Lieutenant Colonel Carr would lead Companies B, G, and M eastward toward the Black Hills before turning south to Sage Creek. Major John J. Upham would lead Companies A, C, and D northwestward up the valley of the South Fork of the Cheyenne before angling southeast. And Merritt himself, leading "I" and "K," still worn from the chase the day before, would backtrack directly up Old Woman's Fork toward Sage Creek. Carr and Upham "were ordered to make a wide detour, scout the country for forty-eight hours, and rejoin headquarters."[27]

The battalions marched as ordered. On July 5 Upham's column encountered rifle pits and the bodies of two dead men. They were thought to be Black Hills-bound prospectors having traveled perhaps from Fort Fetterman, who had been ambushed and killed by Indians. None of the columns saw tribesmen. On the afternoon of the fifth, they began reassembling at the army stockade nestled in the breaks of the Pine Ridge at the head of Sage Creek. Dubbed Camp on Sage Creek, Company H, Twenty-third Infantry, commanded in the field by First Lieutenant George McManis Taylor, had founded and garrisoned this modest Fort Laramie subpost since June 15, primarily safeguarding traffic on the Black Hills Road midway between Fort Laramie and a sister camp located at the mouth of Red Canyon, Dakota, a southwestern entry to the Hills.[28]

As the Fifth rested in its camp adjacent to the infantry stockade, on July 6 a courier arrived from Fort Laramie bearing a seemingly prophetic letter from the post commander. "I have the honor to report," wrote Major Townsend,

> that Subsistance Stores and some forage will start for your command tomorrow morning early, under the escort of Company F 9th Infantry, 1st Lieut. W. W. Rogers 9th Infantry Commanding. The delay in forwarding the necessary supplies had been occasioned by the non-arrival of the train carrying coffee and sugar, which came in this morning. Other supplies, and forage particularly, will be pushed forward as rapid as possible, and surely in time for needed issues.
>
> Your courier had just arrived, and will leave tomorrow with latest mail; due this morning.[29]

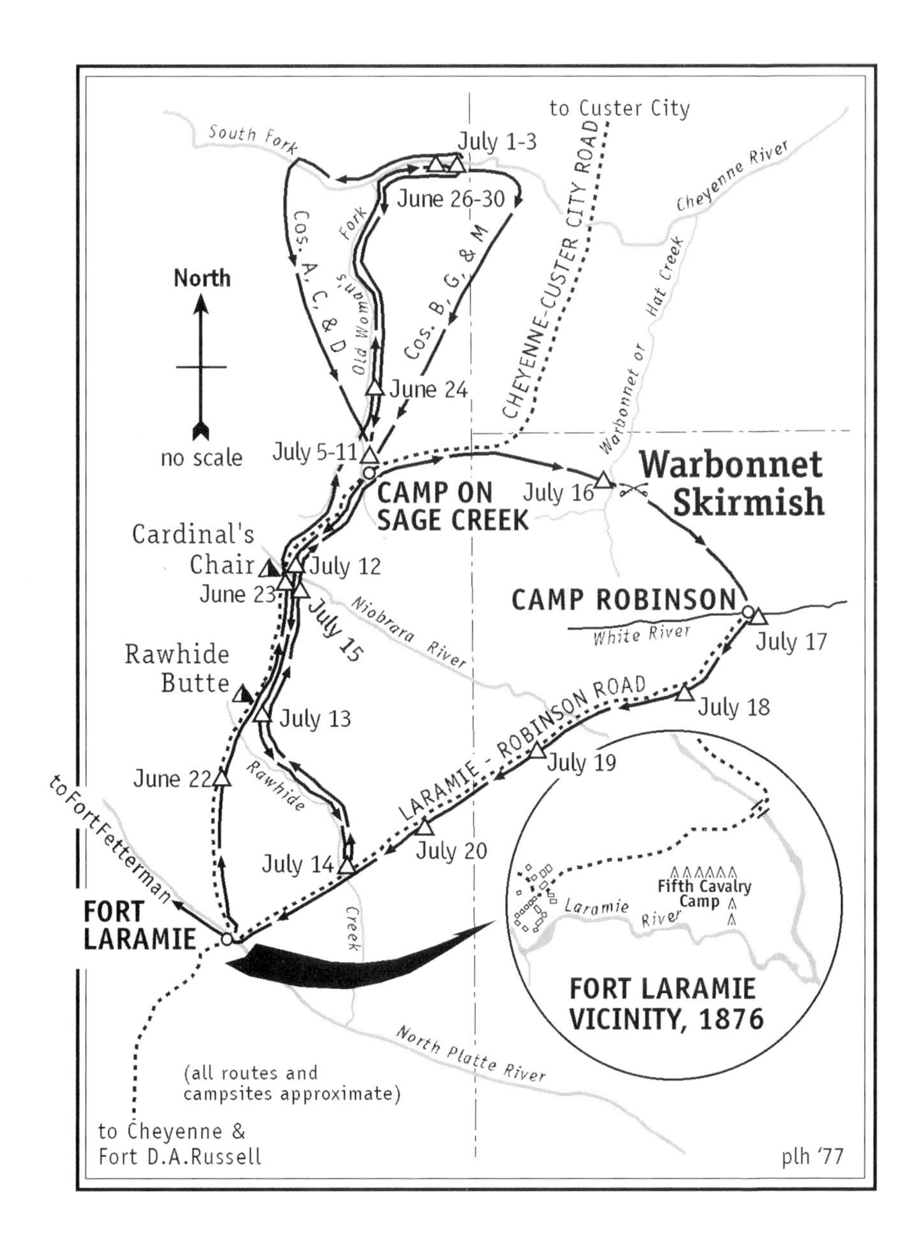

to Custer City
South Fork
July 1-3
June 26-30
Cheyenne River
CHEYENNE-CUSTER CITY ROAD
Cos. A, C, & D
Old Woman's Fork
Cos. B, G, & M
North
Hat Creek
Warbonnet or
June 24
no scale
July 5-11
CAMP ON SAGE CREEK
July 16
Warbonnet Skirmish
Cardinal's Chair
July 12
June 23
July 15
Niobrara River
CAMP ROBINSON
White River
July 17
Rawhide Butte
July 13
LARAMIE - ROBINSON ROAD
July 18
July 19
June 22
Rawhide
to Fort Fetterman
July 20
July 14
Creek
Fifth Cavalry Camp
Laramie River
FORT LARAMIE
FORT LARAMIE VICINITY, 1876
North Platte River
(all routes and campsites approximate)
to Cheyenne & Fort D.A.Russell
plh '77

The "latest mail" arriving at Fort Laramie on July 6 was shocking indeed. The Laramie garrison learned that Custer and nearly half of his Seventh Cavalry Regiment had been annihilated on June 25 at the Little Big Horn River in Montana. Townsend promptly drafted a letter repeating this news for Merritt, gave it to Lieutenant Rogers, escorting the supply train, and ordered him to deliver it to the Fifth Cavalry as expeditiously as practicable. Rogers, in turn, sent a special courier north on the Black Hills Road.[30]

At about mid-morning on July 7, Bill Cody guided the Laramie courier to Merritt's bivouac. There the regiment received the devastating news of Custer's defeat. Surely the assembled officers speculated that they would now be ordered north to Crook. Later that evening, however, First Lieutenant William P. Hall, the Fifth's acting regimental quartermaster, appeared with other orders. Sheridan directed that Merritt should not push toward the Powder River country, but go either to Red Cloud Agency or back to Fort Laramie, whichever in Merritt's judgment he thought best. Merritt elected to remain camped on Sage Creek, where, he concluded, he was centrally located and better able to respond to situations on the road, or at the agencies, Camp Robinson, or Fort Laramie.[31]

Several sorties were ordered forth, but each was fruitless. Carr, evidently still chafing from the change of command, welcomed these opportunities to engage the tribesmen. King, in a letter to his family, wrote, "Carr was wild to do something . . . but Mr. Lo was too much occupied to the northwest to spare more than enough to meet us man for man, which would have been imprudent."[32]

On July 11 the command drew its first beef ration since departing Fort Laramie on June 22. It was "worth its weight in gold," diarist James Frew recorded.[33] The next day, the regiment departed Sage Creek under new orders from Sheridan. The orders were to return to Fort Laramie, refit, and head north by way of Fort Fetterman for Crook's camp in the Big Horn Mountains. After his fight at Rosebud Creek, Montana, on June 17, Crook sat idly along Goose Creek, near present-day Sheridan, Wyoming, adamant in the belief that his only chance for success against the northern Indians would come if he were supported by additional troops, particularly Merritt and his eight cavalry companies. Already Crook commanded twelve hundred effectives, and observers debated his logic in demanding additional troops, yet he successfully delayed any movement until the Fifth Cavalry and others arrived.[34]

By the evening of July 12 Merritt's command was again camped in the shadows of Cardinal's Chair. They had marched some sixteen miles nearer to Fort Laramie. That evening they were caught in a furious thunderstorm, with lightning and hail which lasted most of the night and thoroughly soaked the men. The next day the column moved eighteen miles down the trail and camped by another local landmark, Rawhide Butte. Again, that evening a thundershower pummeled the column.[35]

A curious incident occurred in the regiment during this time. Apparently not all of the Fifth's officer corps was enthusiastic about field service and the prospects of combat. One company commander, Robert A. Wilson of "A," was evidently neither enthusiastic nor afraid to shirk danger at any apparent cost. But Wilson carried one sham too far, was discovered, and then directed to resign his commission or face a court-martial. In a letter to his father dated July 11, King provides details:

> Our swell english dandy Captain who managed to evade all rough duty in Arizona by three successive leaves of absence, obtained Heaven only knows how, was forced to come with us on this trip by the suddenness of the order, and stuck it out tolerably well but a forty hour scout, followed by the sad news of the Custer massacre was too much for him. He was attacked with copious hemorrhage, he said from the lungs, it proved to be from the nose, a lieutenant relieved the "don" from command of his company and he accompanies us back to Laramie, under a cloud.[36]

Wilson's resignation on July 15 was accepted by the President, to take effect on July 29, 1876. Wilson departed the regiment on the fifteenth, returning by way of Fort Laramie. Second Lieutenant Robert London, formally assigned to Company I but detailed to Company A since June 20, assumed command.[37]

On July 14 when but one day's march from Fort Laramie, rumors circulated through the camp that Merritt had received important news from the agencies via Laramie. On July 11 Major Townsend at Fort Laramie had, indeed, received a communication from the commander at Camp Robinson announcing that hundreds of Cheyenne Indians intended to depart the agency for the north. He promptly forwarded the news to Merritt, who received it late on July 13.[38]

When the Fifth broke camp on the fourteenth, it marched southeastward rather than on the trail directly to Fort Laramie, and by noon reached the crossing of the Camp Robinson-Fort Laramie Road and Rawhide Creek. Merritt was anxious to verify the news from Robinson. If, indeed, Northern Cheyenne tribesmen were fleeing the agency in numbers, his duty to check that flight would surely temporarily override his orders to join Crook. The regiment halted at the crossing and Merritt ordered Major Stanton to Camp Robinson and Red Cloud Agency to investigate. Company C, commanded by Captain Emil Adams, was ordered to accompany Stanton as far as the Niobrara River and then commence patrolling the Laramie-Robinson trail.[39]

Stanton arrived at Camp Robinson late on Friday evening, July 14. He conferred with Captain William H. Jordan, Ninth Infantry, commanding the post, and wrote the following dispatch to Merritt:

> Camp Robinson
> Saturday July 15 1876
>
> General
>
> A considerable number of Sioux Warriors left here for north this morning. The Cheyennes are also going—taking women & children. There has been great demand for ammunition for several days, Indians even offering a pony for 30 rounds of cartridges. When the 800 Cheyennes now leaving are gone there will be none left here of that tribe of 2300. All information agrees that at least 900 Sioux warriors are absent from agency, and they are doubtless with Sitting Bull, as there has been much mourning here for bucks killed up there. Indians here report 263 warriors killed in Custer's fight; also that 86 were killed in Crook's fight.
>
> I should say it would be well to move your lines in as near the agency as possible. After Indians get out any distance their chances for slipping by you are much better. The Sage Creek line is too far out—would draw it in 25 or 30 miles, or even more, towards the agency. The Indians think you are still at Sage Creek & along there, and count on getting by you easily. I dont know but it would even be as well to come right here. The agent here is thoroughly stampeded by the threatening bearing of the Indians since the Custer fight, and came near throwing up the sponge and quitting yesterday. Thinks

there are not troops enough here to protect the agency in case of trouble.

I would suggest that Fitzgerald's company be brought in. There is no mail carried on that route now, and no travel. Besides where he is, he is just bait for the Indians in case of an event. The strength of the garrison here, present for duty, is 130 men, and the post, as you know, is very untenable, with so small a force. It should be strengthened rather than weakened, & especially as the company up the canon can do no good there, and would be in imminent danger in case of an outbreak. I would bring it in.

The Indians tell the agent that he had better get out of here, and are very sassy. Everybody seems unsettled and anxious, but how much trouble will come of it all is hard to tell. The principal men of the Sioux are here, with most of women & children. I do not believe they will go away or make much trouble. Little Wound & his tribe (whom Carr thrashed so soundly) are here and say they are not going away.

I will wait here until I hear from you. Send a small escort when you wish me to join. The horses we rode yesterday are well played out & need a day or two's rest. Let me know where you will be, so I can join soon as possible, and also give me any further instructions you may wish or anything you wish done here.

Stanton

General Merritt

P.S. 12. m. It seems now that the Cheyennes left last night—all except a few old men & women. So you will have to hurry up if you catch any of them. About 100 Indians, wounded in Crook's fight, are reported to be distributed among their friends here, and there is much mourning for killed—showing that many Indians from here are with Sitting Bull. I still think it would be well to draw your lines in as near as possible towards the agency. In view of state of affairs here Jordan has ordered Fitzgerald to hold himself in readiness to come in. Indians leaving here will doubtless scatter in any direction, in small parties, to get by you. Let me know where & when to join you.

Stanton

> The Cheyennes have disposed mostly of their lodgepoles, and take their families on ponies.
>
> Maj. Jordan says he would write by this courier but it would only be a repetition of what I have written.[40]

Stanton's dispatch revealed several critical facts. The agency Cheyennes, for instance, still believed that the Fifth Cavalry was encamped on the Powder River Trail, blocking that avenue to the northern camps. At the same time, they were confident of their ability to elude the troops. The perceived weakened and threatened status of Camp Robinson and Red Cloud Agency was also glaring, compelling Stanton to suggest that Fitzgerald's Ninth Infantry company be withdrawn from trail service to bolster the garrison. Michael J. Fitzgerald's Company D had been guarding the Running Water Station on the Sidney-Black Hills Trail south of Camp Robinson since early June, but, ultimately, was not withdrawn to Robinson until July 20.[41]

William Jordan's dispatch was shorter but equally urgent:

> I have the honor to report that I have just received reliable information that about 800 Northern Cheyennes / men women and children / containing about 150 fighting men, and a good many Sioux all belonging to Red Cloud Agency are to leave here tomorrow for the north. Also that "Sitting Bull" heretofore the most friendly and trustworthy of the Sioux Indians at the Agency left for the north on the 11th instant and that it is my belief that a good many Indians have been leaving since the receipt of the news of the disaster of Lieutenant Colonel Custer.[42]

The Stanton and Jordan letters formed the substantive information upon which Merritt planned a course of action. He was still under orders to advance to Crook, but surely his superiors would appreciate the gravity of this circumstance. As he understood it, eight hundred Cheyenne Indians were soon to leave—or had already departed—Red Cloud Agency for the north, wherein were the camps of Crazy Horse and Sitting Bull and the warriors who had destroyed Custer's command. His only logical recourse was to backtrack and intercept the Cheyennes. That he did not dally in coming to that decision is well recorded, but before departing the Rawhide Creek crossing he sent a courier to Robinson to bring on Stanton, and a dispatch to Fort Laramie to signal his intentions.[43]

Merritt's communication was promptly telegraphed to Sheridan in Chicago, who forwarded it to General William T. Sherman, commanding general of the army, in Washington, D. C. "General Merritt has learned," Sheridan's message to Sherman read,

> that eight hundred (800) Cheyennes and a lot of Sioux intend to start today or tomorrow from Red Cloud Agency to join the hostile Indians. His movement to join Crook will be interrupted by an attempt to intercept them; after which his movement to join Crook will be continued. I understand that the number of Indians named includes men, women and children.[44]

To catch the fleeing Cheyennes, Merritt's command would necessarily have to backtrack north over the trail they had so recently traversed, at least as far as the infantry camp at Sage Creek, and then angle east, hopefully to be in front of any outbound Indians. An approach from any other direction would place the cavalrymen behind their foe, and they had already learned that trailing Indians was difficult and unrewarding duty. By 1 P.M. on the fifteenth the Fifth Cavalry was prepared to march. Tended by their original infantry guard from Fort Laramie, and with Lieutenant Hall in charge, Merritt directed that the wagons follow however possible.

Forced marching was grueling business. No time was lost on meals and when hungry, the troopers reached into their haversacks for hardcrackers, a campaign staple. By sunset the column began its descent into the Niobrara or Running Water River valley, and by 10 P.M. reached that watercourse. There the troopers halted, picketed their animals, and briefly rested. They had covered nearly thirty-five miles since departing Rawhide Creek earlier that afternoon. To everyone's amazement, Lieutenant Hall and the supply wagons arrived at midnight.[45]

At 3 A.M. on the sixteenth, Merritt roused his command. The men were allowed time for breakfast, amounting to bacon, coffee, and hardcrackers, and the horses well grained before departing. By 5 A.M. the column was moving again, and by midmorning had crossed the divide between the Niobrara and Cheyenne drainages, where it turned toward Camp on Sage

Creek. Surprised by their return, First Lieutenant Taylor and the men of Company H, Twenty-third Infantry, welcomed the Fifth as it approached their little fortification shortly after 10 A.M. The column spent about an hour at the cantonment, where the men were allowed to prepare a meal. When Hall's wagons arrived cartridge crates were opened and everyone stuffed thimble belts, pockets, and saddlebags with extra carbine and pistol ammunition. Because Merritt intended on advancing well ahead of his supply train when the march resumed, he had his companies rationed for three days. He wished that the wagons would follow, however, and bolstered the Ninth Infantry escort by commandeering three squads from Taylor's Twenty-third Infantry company.[46]

After barely more than an hour's halt, the Fifth was marching again. Merritt intended on reaching that point where the Indian trail crossed Warbonnet Creek, just across the Wyoming-Nebraska line. He led the column at a pace of about four and a half miles per hour; anything more would stir clouds of dust and betray his approach. The column was bound in an easterly direction, at first following the Black Hills Road, but soon veering from it and proceeding across rolling, treeless prairie.[47]

At sunset, with the southernmost Black Hills looming distinctly on their far left and the sinuous Pine Ridge on their right, the command sighted the winding fringe of green cottonwood trees marking Warbonnet Creek. The column's scouts reported the Indian trail in view, but with no Indian on it. By 8 P.M. Merritt dismounted his cavalrymen on the winding course of the sluggish little creek. They had covered eighty-five miles in thirty-one hours, a noteworthy forced march by any standard and a feat long remembered by the regiment. Most important of all, the Cheyenne Indians had not eluded the command.[48]

Chapter 2

The Skirmish

MERRITT PERMITTED A FEW SMALL COOKING FIRES in the Warbonnet Creek bivouac on the evening of July 16. Most of the men had not eaten since departing the Sage Creek palisade eight hours earlier. Soon after the command halted, Lieutenant Forbush, the column's adjutant, detailed Mason's Company K for guard and picket duty. Company K's second officer, Charles King, balked when hearing the news since he had been on similar duty the night before, having been assigned with Company G. Still, the anticipation of Indian contact the next morning was incentive enough to accept the assignment without protest. As the remainder of the command settled in for the night, King concealed men in depressions and hollows, where they could best observe objects against the night sky. Picket duty was a demanding responsibility, and with an already exhausted force it was all the more challenging. Several times when King made rounds checking the guards, he came upon sleeping men. Though naturally required to rebuke the violators, it was doubtless done with a sympathetic tongue.[49]

Merritt left orders that he be awakened at 3:30 A.M., Monday morning, July 17. Punctually, King obliged his commander, reporting "all quiet, except a suspicious yelping of coyotes," and then returned to an outpost on the southeastern perimeter.[50] As contrasts on the horizon grew distinct against the brightening sky, King discerned two pronounced conical hills rising in his front, the first some ninety feet high and about three hundred yards away, and the second four hundred yards distant. Because they cut off his view of the land beyond, he moved his own outpost to the southernmost hill, and positioned Private Christian Madsen of Company A on the northern one, one hundred yards closer to the camp.

In the breaking light King was able to study the varied topography. The dry grass of mid-July covered the land all around with a distinct tan. Behind him, to the west, he could see the rolling hills that the regiment had crossed the evening before. To the north, King could follow the winding tree line marking Warbonnet Creek, as it coursed its way to the South Fork of the Cheyenne, well out of sight in the distance. On the far northern horizon, however, he could see the fringe of the Black Hills at its southernmost extreme. In the opposite direction, to the south, King could see the heralded Pine Ridge, some twelve miles away. This sinewy, pine-covered escarpment stretched from east-central Wyoming, through northwestern Nebraska, and into the Dakota Territory. To the southeast, from which direction the Indians were expected, King could plainly see gently rolling, grass-covered ridges and valleys. These, the Cheyennes would likely use in their flight from the Red Cloud Agency, the tribe's unofficial home. Forming the distant limits of King's view to the southeast was the Pine Ridge again.

By 4:00 A.M. the Fifth was stirring. Fires were not permitted this morning and the troopers made do with cold coffee and salt pork from the night before, if anything of the sort remained, and otherwise with what King called a "hard tack breakfast."[51] The regiment was primed. The seven companies tallied some 330 enlisted men, plus sixteen officers, Doctor Powell, Bill Cody, and Cody's scouting companions, Jonathan White, Little Bat Garnier, and the two mixed-bloods.

Back on the hill King and Corporal Thomas W. Wilkinson of Company K anxiously watched the ridges and valleys to the southeast. At about 4:15 A.M., King remembered, Corporal Wilkinson pointed to a now plainly lighted ridge and exclaimed:

"Look, lieutenant—there are Indians!"[52]

The corporal had sighted a group of young Cheyenne warriors who had ridden over the head of a ravine some two miles away and were slowly making their way toward the command. And in a motion difficult for King and Wilkinson to immediately comprehend, the warriors were seen darting half way up the shallow ravine they were traveling, always peering west.

These warriors, including Beaver Heart, Buffalo Road, and Yellow Hair, were mostly members of Morning Star's band of Northern Cheyenne Indians.

True to reports, Morning Star had learned of the Custer battle and was leading followers from the agency to friends and allies in the Powder River country. On the night of the sixteenth his band had camped seven miles from Warbonnet Creek, and at the break of day on the seventeenth scouts were sent ahead to look for soldiers.[53]

The Cheyennes, indeed, were watching soldiers, but not the seven companies of the Fifth Cavalry, who were obscured by the tall cutbanks of the creek. Instead, they had spotted the tireless Lieutenant Hall and his wagon train. Hall had pushed forward through most of the night, aiming to join Merritt. Now, unknown to him, he had been discovered by Cheyenne warriors who were spoiling for a fight.

Merritt was notified immediately when the warriors were spotted and quickly joined the pickets on the southern hill, as did Carr, Captain Sumner of D Company, and several others. As they peered cautiously southeastward, other Indians came into view. By 5 A.M., dozens of warriors were huddled about a mile and a half from the cavalrymen, all intently watching Hall's canvas-topped army wagons.

Merritt ordered Carr to have the seven companies saddle up and close on the cutbanks lining the east side of the creek. The men had finished their morning duties and had spent recent minutes wiping trail dust off their weapons, checking cartridges in their Colt revolvers, and loading their Springfield carbines. On whispered commands and with soldier precision, they mounted and closed on the creek. The ravine in which the Cheyenne warriors were concealed led in a westerly direction toward Warbonnet Creek. The soldiers figured that somewhere on the course of that broad bottom or its flanks they would face the Indians. The warriors, in turn, saw only the wagons advancing on the distant horizon.

Bill Cody was late in joining the observers on the hill. With Merritt's consent and perhaps even at his urging, he had ventured east before daybreak and had discovered the location of the Cheyenne camp. But before he could pass on the information, King and others were already watching the Cheyenne scouts.[54]

The scene was colorful and poignant in the extreme, the combatants brilliantly attired as if, somehow, anticipating history's embrace. King, ever the deliberate wordsmith, wrote how Indian "warfare was never more beautiful." "On you come," he wrote of the Cheyenne warriors, "your swift, agile, ponies springing down the winding ravine, the rising sun gleaming on your trailing war bonnets, on silver armlets, necklace, gorget; on brilliant painted shield and beaded legging; on naked body and beardless face, stained most vivid vermilion."[55] Yellow Hair, foremost among the advancing warriors, wore a feather bonnet, tin bracelets, a charm, a beaded belt wherein was tucked a scalp of yellow or blonde hair, thus deriving his name, and, as was later discovered, a breechcloth fashioned from a cotton American flag.[56]

Cody, too, had dressed uniquely for the occasion, deliberately seizing the opportunity to validate the scouting outfit he favored on Combination Show stages. Before starting out that morning, he dressed in showman's garb. Cynthia Capron had noted his wearing a scarlet shirt at Fort Laramie, when the regiment passed through at the end of June. He wore it again this morning. It was red silk with billowy sleeves and a single row of silver bullet buttons ornamenting the placket. His trousers were black velvet, flaring below the knees and decorated with criss-cross braid on the thighs and more braid and bullet buttons down the outer seams. Cody's brown leather belt was doublewide and featured a large, rectangular, silver-washed buckle, commonly seen later in the Wild West arenas and photographs. And crowning his head was a large, floppy-brimmed, brushed beaver fur hat. King called the outfit a Mexican vaquero costume, and by whatever name, it was outlandish in the extreme, but a perfect statement for an actor seizing the Warbonnet stage.[57]

On the hill, Cody was the first to notice peculiar activity among the Indians. In an excited manner they motioned toward the wagons. Then suddenly about a dozen warriors started down the ravine toward the Fifth Cavalrymen. Quizzically, the officers wondered what was up, but in an instant the Cheyennes' intent became obvious.

Looking back toward the wagons, the men on the hill could see two cavalrymen advancing ahead of Hall's cavalcade. These men, later identified as Privates Harry Anderson and Gordon W. Keith, both of Company C, Fifth Cavalry, carried dispatches for Merritt. Company C had departed its station along the Laramie-Robinson Road on July 16 and followed the regiment's trail. Anderson and Keith were sent ahead to announce their movement. But at the moment, completely unknown to them, Cheyenne warriors were hurrying to cut them off. And, unknown to the warriors, seven companies of Fifth Cavalry were watching and planning an even greater surprise.[58]

Cody recognized the unfolding opportunity in an instant. A handful of men, he reckoned, could overpower the warriors advancing down the ravine and thus turn the rest to flight. Merritt agreed, and as most of the party slipped down the hill, he called back to King telling him to watch the Indians until they closed in, and then announce the attack.

In King's words,

> I am the only man left on the top of the hill. My hat is off. Only the top of my head and my binoculars are visible above the crest and I am not seen. Merritt and two staff officers, Forbush and J. Hayden Pardee . . . are crouching just out of sight down the slope. Nearby are Sergeant Schreiber and Corporal Wilkinson.[59]

All around, adrenaline flowed in the cavalry troopers, who nervously fidgeted with their holsters and had advanced their carbines. Farther to the south, near where the Indians' ravine opened into Warbonnet Creek, Cody was poised with Jonathan White, another of the scouts, and half a dozen men from Company K. Everyone watched Lieutenant King.

King waited until the warriors closed to within ninety yards of Warbonnet Creek, and then shouted down,

> "NOW, lads, in with you!"[60]

Cody was first into the swale, the shallow, sinuous, grassy drainage emptying into the creek. He galloped forward to within thirty yards of the Indians, as he later recollected, where he raised his rifle and fired at the foremost warrior. The Indian's horse fell at once, killed by Cody, toppling the as yet unnamed warrior, who was wounded in the leg by the same shot. Almost simultaneously Cody and his own horse went down, the mount having stumbled in an animal burrow. Cody recovered quickly, as did the warrior, and they fired at each other. The warrior's shot missed its mark, but Cody's bullet struck the Indian in the breast, killing him instantly.[61]

Cody dashed forward to the dead Indian, who was lying face down next to his horse. He dismounted, approached the body, jerked off the Indian's feather bonnet, drew his own knife, and scalped him. As soldiers rode by during the unfolding action, Cody raised the warrior's scalp and bonnet and proclaimed loudly:

> "The first scalp for Custer."[62]

Cody soon told an exaggerated version of this simple but dangerous encounter. When reenacting the killing and scalping of Yellow Hair that fall in a new stage production, *The Red Right Hand; or, Buffalo Bill's First Scalp for Custer,* his friend and playwright Prentiss Ingraham added embellishments that transformed the straightforward action of deft marksmanship into a heroic duel. Certainly for the close quarters of the stage, having two warriors square off, acknowledge one another, fire shots, and, as Yellow Hair reeled, having Cody pounce upon him, knife in hand, and drive the "keen-edged weapon to its hilt in his heart," amounted to dramatic and colorful scripting. But it never happened that way at Warbonnet Creek. No one witnessed a duel of any sort and many were later asked. Yellow Hair did not recognize Cody at the onset and sing out in his Cheyenne tongue, "I know you, Pa-he-haska; if you want to fight, come ahead and fight me," Ingraham's lurid prose and Cody's own repetition of that scenario in his autobiography notwithstanding. In a close range, adrenaline-filled exchange of shots, Cody could have been killed at Warbonnet, but, instead, Yellow Hair was. That was Great Sioux War heroics enough.[63]

Those few shots in the swale initiated action on several fronts. The warriors remaining back a mile or so immediately started forward to rescue their seemingly trapped companions. At the quartermaster train, when Hall heard the firing, he ordered his infantry escort out of the wagons and into skirmish formation. From the hill, Merritt ordered Company K onto the high ground north of the ravine to check the advancing warriors. And down below, Cody's companions charged the stunned Cheyenne scouts who accompanied Yellow Hair and scattered them before any other injuries were inflicted.[64]

As King's Company K gained the flats off the creek bottom, he scurried down from his lookout, mounted, and took a position with his platoon. With Major Mason in charge, and employing maneuvering direct from their *Cavalry Tactics* manual, the company spread into open order and charged. Simultaneously, Captain Montgomery's Company B took position on "K's" right, while Captain Kellogg's Company I came into line on the left.[65] These three companies, numbering 147 men, chased the Indians in close quarters for nearly three miles. In their hurried flight, the warriors littered the prairie with blankets, foodstuffs, and anything else that could be spared, except for weapons and ammunition.[66]

Mason quickly realized that the Indians had been turned and were retiring

Warbonnet Creek Skirmish Site, looking west. This is the setting that Morning Star's scouts viewed at daybreak on July 17. Lieutenant King and others were perched on the small hill at center and the Fifth Cavalry was secreted beneath the cutbanks of Warbonnet Creek, beyond. Courtesy of Paul L. Hedren

Warbonnet Creek, looking south-southwest. Scattered cottonwood trees mark the winding course of Warbonnet Creek. The dark tone across the horizon is the heralded Pine Ridge. Courtesy of James Hatzell

The "First Scalp for Custer." This woodcut by T. "True" Williams appeared in Cody's 1879 autobiography, *The Life of Hon. William F. Cody,* and is the first artistic rendition of the "first scalp" episode. Dozens more by artists known and unknown followed during and after Cody's lifetime, making it one of the most frequently illustrated episodes of the Great Sioux War. Courtesy of the Nebraska State Historical Society

Cody-Yellow Hair Fight Site. Cody killed and scalped the Cheyenne scout Yellow Hair in the proximity of the monument at center. The monument commemorating the Fifth Cavalry's participation in the Warbonnet Skirmish juts from the hill on the right horizon. Courtesy of James Hatzell

Trophies collected by Cody from Yellow Hair. Cody exhibited this collection of articles belonging to Yellow Hair when his Combination Show, *The Red Right Hand,* toured the nation in 1876–77. The artifacts generated the occasional dismay of press and clergy but also abundant attention. Courtesy of the Buffalo Bill Historical Center; P.69.39

Red Cloud Agency in 1876. Near here on the evening of July 17, the Fifth Cavalry concluded its chase of Morning Star's followers and wrote reports of the episode. Courtesy of the Nebraska State Historical Society; RG2063-PH:16-3

at a good pace to Red Cloud Agency. Keeping the pursued in sight, he halted the battalion and waited for Merritt and the other companies. Back at the creek, Merritt and Carr, in turn, awaited the arrival of the escort wagons and then rationed the companies for two additional days. Merritt intended to chase the tribesmen and was unsure when his command would access its wagons again.[67]

In the swale Cody was radiant in his personal success. His shots had felled the only Indian killed in the quick, surprise encounter. Before abandoning the field, Cody added Yellow Hair's quirt, weapons, and a handful of other trophies to his cache, which he bundled up and tied to his saddle. Years later, others claimed to be Yellow Hair's slayer, but none of the assertions stands careful scrutiny. Bill Cody, indeed, killed a Cheyenne scout whose name was not yet even known. And he took the Indian's scalp, likely as atonement for the death of his friend, Custer.[68]

One Fifth Cavalry participant at Warbonnet Creek, Sergeant John Hamilton of Sumner's Company D, later provided unique details on Yellow Hair's death scene. From the southern hill, Hamilton, Sumner, and others witnessed the opening of the fight, watching Cody and Yellow Hair fire at each other and then tumble from their horses. At that point Hamilton and the others scampered off the hill to rejoin their respective companies as Merritt deployed the troops. Company D was not immediately forwarded into line to chase the warriors, however, but held at the creek. When Hamilton's company finally advanced, their route took them directly past Yellow Hair's body, and a situation there obliged him and a private, Christian Ahrens, to dismount on the spot to fix a pack mule saddle that had loosened. There Hamilton had a long, discerning look at Yellow Hair, "lying on his stomach, head on folded or bent arms, his scalp was taken, he had on his person a paint bag, a scalp of hair, yellow color of some young woman, tin bracelets on arms, a charm, wampum belt, war feathers, and a cotton American flag as a breech cloth."[69]

In Morning Star's camp, well back from the engagement, the villagers heard the scattered shots at Warbonnet. Presuming that their front was blocked, they hurriedly struck their camp and started for Red Cloud.[70] As the troopers advanced, they passed through the site. Merritt reported later that the Cheyennes had left behind four lodges standing and several hundred pounds of provisions.

Distributed across a wide front, the Fifth Cavalry chased Morning Star's

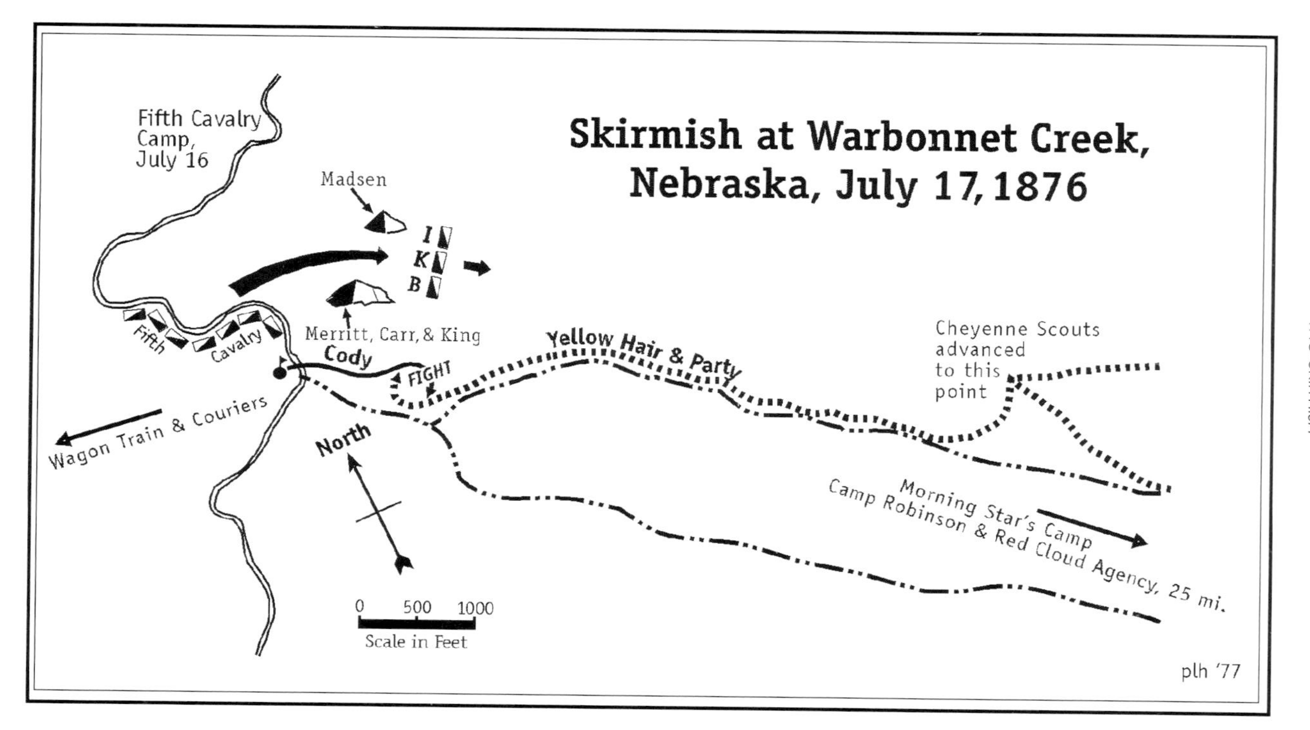
Skirmish at Warbonnet Creek,
Nebraska, July 17, 1876
Fifth Cavalry Camp, July 16
Madsen
I
K
B
Merritt, Carr, & King
Fifth Cavalry
Cody
FIGHT
Yellow Hair & Party
Cheyenne Scouts advanced to this point
Wagon Train & Couriers
North
0 500 1000
Scale in Feet
Morning Star's Camp
Camp Robinson & Red Cloud Agency, 25 mi.
plh '77

followers for nearly thirty miles across the breaks north of and paralleling the Pine Ridge to the proximity of Red Cloud Agency. The Fifth's sole casualty in the affair occurred when a private, James Jeffers of D Company, was hurt when his horse slipped and tumbled down an embankment.[71]

The Cheyenne trail came to within four miles of Red Cloud and then veered east toward the Spotted Tail Agency, forty miles distant. Confident that this band of would-be warriors was again within the control of Indian agents, Merritt turned his weary troopers toward Red Cloud and they were soon camped at the agency. The cavalrymen were worn, but feeling immensely successful. They had, in their impression, turned back hundreds of potentially warlike Indians—any and all of whom they might have faced later on. The irony of it all became apparent a short while later when the men were preparing evening rations and were joined by many of the tribesmen they chased throughout the day. The Indians had come to talk it over.[72]

In the few remaining hours of daylight and through some of the morning of the eighteenth the officers busily prepared reports on the episode, while others in the column seized the opportunity to write letters home. Merritt's official report was telegraphed to Fort Laramie on the eighteenth and relayed quickly to anxious audiences in Chicago and Washington. In his words,

> I moved by forced march to the main northwest trail on Indian Creek. In thirty five hours my command made about seventy five miles reaching the trail Sunday evening about nine o'clock P.M. The trail showed no large parties had passed north.
>
> At daylight yesterday morning I saddled up to move on the trail toward the agency, at the same time a party of seven indians were discovered near the command moving with the intentions of cutting off two couriers who were approaching from Sage Creek. A party was sent out to cut these off killing one of them. The command then moved out at once after the other indians seen in this direction and pursued them, they escaped leaving four lodges and several hundred pounds of provisions behind. After scouring the country thoroughly in our vicinity we moved at a distance of twenty-five miles to the Northwest of the Agency, the indians broke camp and fled in so that we did not succeed in catching any of them. The trail was much worn and the indications were that hundreds of Indians were driven in by

> our movement. From repeated reports which I cannot give in this dispatch I was certain of striking the Cheyennes. To accomplish this I worked hard to get on the trail taking Infantry along to guard the wagons and to fight if necessary. The reports from this point led me to believe that many warriors were with the Cheyennes. I am now satisfied the number of Indians leaving the Agency are exaggerated in the reports and I am certain that not a hundred indians or rather ponies all told have gone north on the main trail in the last ten days. The Cheyennes who we drove in yesterday took refuge on the reservation toward Spotted Tail. If they leave again I think it will be to go south, to the Agencies as they seem to be thoroughly frightened out of the northern trip.
>
> Our appearance on Indian and Hat Creeks was a complete surprise to the indians in that vicinity but those further in were informed by runners so that they got out of the way. I have just received your dispatches of the fifteenth. I will move without delay to Fort Laramie and as soon as possible move to join Crook. My men and horses are very tired but a few days reasonable marching with full forage will make them all right.
>
> Merritt[73]

Carr was less effusive over the regiment's success on the seventeenth. With an evident bitterness, in fact, he wrote his wife that he wished he could write a report so large as Merritt's on such small material. "There were not over 30 Indians in sight at any one time," he wrote,

> and we had over 400 men. There were a few sacks of flour destroyed, three Indians killed, 12 ponies captured and a few went back to the Agency—probably to go North and depredate the settlements. The animals of the Command are much injured by the trip. Many sore backs and the mules so much that they can hardly pull the wagons.[74]

Bill Cody, meanwhile, sent a chatty letter to his wife, Louisa, wherein he, too, recounted the previous day's activity. At Red Cloud he had learned the name of the Indian killed, which came to him mistranslated as Yellow Hand.[75] Wrote Bill:

Red Cloud Agency,
July 18th '76

My Darling Lulu

We have come in here for rations. We have had a fight. I killed Yellow Hand a Cheyenne Chief in a single-handed fight. You will no doubt hear of it through the paper. I am going as soon as I reach Fort Laramie the place we are heading for now send the war bonnet, shield, bridle, whip, arms and his scalp to Kerngood to put up in his window. I will write Kerngood to bring it up to the house so that you can show it to the neighbors. We are now ordered to join Gen. Crook and will be there in two weeks. Write me at once to Fort Fetterman, Wyoming. My health is not very good. I have worked myself to death. Although I have shot at lots of Indians I have only one scalp I can call my own that fellow I fought single handed in sight of our command and the cheers that went up when he fell was deafening. Well, Lulu, I have no more time to write now. Will write from Laramie to everybody and long letters.

Good-bye my Lulu, a thousand kisses to all from your hubby,

Willie.

Lulu, we have lost General Carr. General Merritt has taken command as he ranks Carr.[76]

Cody had, indeed, assembled a fine collection of Yellow Hair trophies that he boxed and shipped to his old friend, Moses Kerngood, in Rochester, New York, which was then the Cody family's residence. Cody also recounted later that when Yellow Hair's father learned of his son's death and that weapons, ornaments, and other paraphernalia had been collected from the scene, he offered four mules for it all, but Cody demurred. Instead, the Yellow Hair artifacts were soon displayed in show house windows and on stages themselves as Cody toured his *Red Right Hand* show during the winter and spring of 1876 and 1877.[77]

One area newspaper, the *Cheyenne Daily Leader*, quickly picked up news of Merritt's victory. The July 20 lead on the Warbonnet story read:

The reinforcements for Gen. Sitting Bull from Red Cloud agency,

> were checked in their march yesterday by the Fifth Cavalry. The Cheyennes and Sioux scattered to the four winds, Gen. Merritt was unable to follow the warriors, and to-day, probably the agency Indians are again en route for Sitting Bull's camp. It is a pity that only "one good Indian" is the result of this campaign.

The editors then provided a complete transcription of Merritt's report, likely pirated from the telegrapher at Fort D. A. Russell.

Merritt was, of course, still under orders to join Crook and he intended to move just as quickly as his wagon train caught up with him. He and his command anticipated a layover at Camp Robinson for at least a day before Hall arrived. To their astonishment, however, the indefatigable quartermaster guided his train in at noon on the eighteenth. With supplies at hand, Merritt allowed two hours for preparation and then commenced the return to Fort Laramie.

The journey to Laramie was without complication. The command started at 2:30 P.M. on July 18 and marched ten miles southwest. Following marches of twenty-five miles on the nineteenth, twenty-eight miles on the twentieth, and a final thirty miles on the twenty-first, the Fifth Cavalry arrived at Fort Laramie. There they were joined shortly by Company C, which had been traveling in the wake of the main column since the sixteenth.

While at Fort Laramie Lieutenant King, at Cody's request, drafted a news story for the *New York Herald*. It reported in rather modest terms the whole Warbonnet Creek episode. The *Herald*, on the same day, July 23, and on the same page, reported on the inactivity of General Crook, who was, so the story went, awaiting the arrival of the Fifth Cavalry before making any "aggressive" moves.[78]

Merritt and the Fifth Cavalry did not tarry at Fort Laramie. They resupplied and shod horses on July 22, and at 6:00 A.M. on the twenty-third, commenced their delayed march north to General Crook. For them, as for all troops in the field in the summer of 1876, the long, demanding, and still largely unsuccessful campaign dragged on.

Chapter 3

Assessing Warbonnet Creek

FOR MANY, THE SMALL EPISODE at Warbonnet Creek, Nebraska, occurring on July 17, 1876, during the protracted course of the Great Sioux War, is easily forgotten. Only one Indian was killed in the brief encounter at daybreak, and no soldiers, and the Cheyennes intercepted that day merely bided their time near Red Cloud Agency before finding another opportunity to flee and join kinsmen and allies in Wyoming and Montana. Many of these same people, in fact, fought soldiers again in 1876, but the battle occurring on the Red Fork of the Powder River in the southern Big Horn Mountains on November 25 had dire consequences. Morning Star's and Little Wolf's village was destroyed in that fight and Cheyenne casualties were numerous. Never again, in fact, would Northern Cheyenne material culture reach the richness and splendor known by the people before that bitter wintry day.[79]

The army rightly viewed the Warbonnet skirmish as a welcome success despite its seemingly modest nature. The great campaign of 1876 was meant to resolve lingering issues with the Sioux and eventually their allies, and before Warbonnet the army knew only proportionally greater defeat. Warbonnet did not signal the end of the Great Sioux War, which waged on for ten more months, but the clash closed that legacy of defeat. Afterwards, the army pressed its war against the Sioux and Cheyennes at Slim Buttes, Cedar Creek, Powder River, Wolf Mountains, Little Muddy Creek, and a scattering of places in between, and broke the resolve of the northern people. By the spring of 1877 most tribesmen bore witness to the army's so-called "Rule of 1876" by obligingly surrendering themselves and all their weapons and horses at the agencies. Others fled to Canada, only momentarily prolonging an inevitable end. Many of the Cheyenne people engaged at Warbonnet Creek, and later in the Big Horns, surrendered at Camp Robinson on April 21, 1877, closing their participation in the Great Sioux War.[80]

Of the white protagonists at Warbonnet Creek, two men, Charles King and Bill Cody, successfully capitalized on the fight, and largely because of them we remember the moment and ponder its meaning. King was already a driven wordsmith, who for years dutifully maintained a daily diary and was the author of one as yet unpublished novel, inkling the tide that followed. He recounted the Warbonnet action repeatedly, first for Cody at Fort Laramie in the *New York Herald* dispatch, then in an episode in a 1879–80 newspaper series on the war appearing in his hometown paper, the *Milwaukee Sentinel*, and, most important, in his immensely successful memoir of the Fifth Cavalry's service in the Great Sioux War, the book *Campaigning With Crook*.[81] *Campaigning* was reprinted no fewer than nine times during King's life, and remains in print and widely read even to this day. The action leading to Warbonnet Creek, and the clash itself, were prominently featured. King outlived most Warbonnet participants and in later years enjoyed visibility as an authoritative voice on Cody, the Old Army, and the army's battles and skirmishes, sometimes to his chagrin, as Don Russell noted in his introduction to the present book.[82]

Cody, meanwhile, almost immediately fashioned his own unique version of the fight for the Combination Show, titled *The Red Right Hand; or, Buffalo Bill's First Scalp for Custer*, which he presented to American audiences from coast to coast during the winter of 1876–77. For dramatic purposes, the clash with Yellow Hair became a manly hand-to-hand duel instead of quick and deft long-range shooting. Cody echoed *The Red Right Hand* "duel" line in his autobiography, first published in 1879. Artists, meanwhile, fixated on the duel and the "first scalp for Custer" consequence, fashioning renditions of the episode by the score, at first to illustrate versions of Cody's oft-reprinted autobiography or yearly Wild West printed programs, and then, following his death, to recognize one of the signal moments in his life. Whether reenacting the duel, illustrating a book, or memorializing the showman, Cody's "first scalp for Custer" became a legacy he created but then could never escape, and one with qualities that linger to the present.[83]

Chapter 4

Warbonnet Creek Battlefield: Then and Now

THE TRANQUIL, ROLLING PRAIRIE of the Warbonnet Creek skirmish site has changed very little since the day Merritt's Fifth Cavalrymen surprised and defeated Morning Star's Cheyenne warriors. The grasses still turn a lush green in the spring; the cottonwood trees still shed cotton-like seed in the early summer; and the sluggish little stream, often referred to these days as Hat Creek, still winds northward to the South Fork of the Cheyenne River.[84]

But the history of this field from 1876 to the present is quite unlike that of many other noteworthy Indian wars battlefields. While the sites of the Little Big Horn battle, the Fetterman fight, Gibbon's Big Hole battle, and the Wounded Knee massacre have been visited, marked, and studied from the very beginning, the scene of the little Warbonnet engagement was neglected and seemingly even lost for more than fifty years. This is not to suggest that the site was never used because it certainly was; but while ranchers grazed cattle, a town grew nearby, and a pioneer fort was erected on the field's most prominent landmark, apparently no one realized that these activities took place on already significant ground.

Within a few years of the cessation of the Great Sioux War, cattlemen and homesteaders flooded northwestern Nebraska. With this influx came settlements, and one, Montrose, was founded within a quarter mile of the Warbonnet field. By the mid-1880s this small burg had grown to include a general store, post office, church, blacksmith shop, school, law office, and sixty-five residents.[85]

Cody Monument at Warbonnet Creek. This cobblestone monument erected in 1934 commemorates Buffalo Bill's participation in the Skirmish at Warbonnet Creek and his taking of the infamous "first scalp for Custer." Courtesy of Paul L. Hedren

▶ **Fifth Cavalry Monument at Warbonnet Creek. This cobblestone obelisk atop the hill commanding the Warbonnet Skirmish scene was erected in 1934, and reconstructed in 1999 after being largely obliterated in a lightening storm.** Courtesy of Paul L. Hedren

▼ **Dedication of the Fifth Cavalry Monument in 1934. Christian Madsen, center left, a veteran of the 1876 skirmish, and Mrs. Johnny Baker, center right, wife of Cody's so-called foster son, headlined dedication ceremonies for the Warbonnet Creek monuments on September 6, 1934.** Courtesy of the Nebraska State Historical Society; RG3004-PH:83

By 1890 these settlers were captured by the general panic enveloping most of northern Plains Indian country when the ghost dancing scare, particularly emanating from the various Sioux reservations, reached epidemic proportions. Fearful of a general outbreak and associated bloodshed, the Montrose villagers constructed a fortress on the nearest usable hill—the same hill coincidentally used by Merritt, King, and Cody in 1876. With shovels and teams they dug a circular trench near the top, and a twenty by thirty-five-foot underground room along the southern slope. Dubbed "Fort Montrose," this fortification was meant be a place of refuge from Indian trouble that, in the end, never appeared.[86]

The push to discover and mark the Warbonnet Creek skirmish site finally materialized in the late 1920s in an effort orchestrated by Robert S. Ellison of Casper, and J. B. Griffith, Sr., Al Rundquist, and Ralph Olinger, of Lusk, Wyoming. Ellison had been actively marking Wyoming's historic sites with the Wyoming Landmark Commission, and since some records indicated that the Warbonnet site was in that state, Ellison considered it a location his commission ought to acknowledge. The collegial Wyomingites formed a loose-knit organization dubbed "The Amalgamated Association of Hunters of the Spot Where Buffalo Bill Killed Yellow Hand," and commenced the search.[87]

The "Amalgamated Association" began their quest relying principally upon Charles King's account of the affair appearing in *Campaigning With Crook*. The group spent most of the summer of 1929 in futile searches. They confronted dozens of confusions, especially relating to local place names. They located one site in South Dakota that had many of the requisite features, but it proved to be too far from Fort Robinson. Later, after following still-visible wagon tracks that the searchers concluded had been left by Quartermaster Hall's train (but which actually was a segment of the Black Hills Road), they came to believe that the fight took place in Nebraska, quite close to the Montrose hamlet. Working with additional details, plus sketch maps, provided by Charles King, the party located a site with all the necessary qualities. But they sought verification.[88]

In October 1929 King, then eighty-five-years-old and in precarious health, was persuaded to visit Lusk. He traveled the Chicago and Northwestern Railroad —the Cowboy Line—across Nebraska to eastern Wyoming and was met by the Amalgamated Association, plus retired Brigadier General William C. Brown and C. B. Hardin, both of Denver. Together the group traveled northeast to the site. King, exhausted from the travel, failed to identify the field. Some of the landmarks were correct, he allowed, but "the trees were too big."[89]

Undismayed, Griffith and Ellison assembled an even larger party in July 1930. King again traveled from Milwaukee to join another surviving participant, Christian Madsen, who journeyed from Guthrie, Oklahoma. Also joining the party were Johnny Baker, so-called foster son of Buffalo Bill, and General Brown. Upon arriving at the Montrose site, Madsen readily declared it the correct location of their fight fifty-four years earlier. From the southern hill, he pointed out the bivouac of each cavalry company and where Merritt slept during the night of July 16. Several months later, after considerable reflection and study, King also concluded that they had visited the correct site. "Madsen has a better recollection than I had," he remarked.[90]

Over the next several years an effort was made to mark the battlefield. Johnny Baker's wife, Olive, funded one monument commemorating Buffalo Bill's encounter with Yellow Hair. Madsen, meanwhile, led a subscription effort that raised enough money to build a second monument commemorating the Fifth Cavalry's participation in the skirmish.

Both native rock memorials were dedicated on September 6, 1934. King, who had died a year and a half earlier at age eighty-eight, and Johnny Baker, also deceased, were the only principal searchers absent. Madsen, himself eighty-four years old and nearly the last survivor, was present at the ceremonies, as was Olive Baker, General Brown, and dignitaries from Nebraska and Wyoming. The official program was highlighted by addresses from Addison E. Sheldon, superintendent of the Nebraska State Historical Society, and Madsen, who related experiences from the 1876 campaign.[91]

Both monuments survive today as silent witnesses to the events occurring at dawn, July 17, 1876. The Cody monument received a welcome repointing in 1999, the same year that a clutch of enthusiasts dubbed the "Friends of the Warbonnet Battlefield" reconstructed the Fifth Cavalry monument that was largely obliterated by a lightning strike in the summer of 1997. The original foundation and cobble base survived, but the 1934 bronze plate disappeared and was necessarily replaced. Fortunately, many of the monument's original cobblestones were immediately salvaged and returned in 1999 to be incorporated into a faithful reconstruction.[92] Elsewhere, human changes to the landscape are fading away. The trenches and dugout of Fort Montrose, for instance, are only faintly visible and continually melt into the hillside. Traces of the little hamlet of Montrose are nearly gone as well, aside from a small Catholic Church and neighboring cemetery occasionally used by local ranch families. For modern partisans having the time to trek up the hill used so advantageously by Fifth Cavalrymen, now more than one hundred and twenty-eight years ago, one can almost hear Lieutenant King shout out,

"NOW, lads, in with you!"

Plaque on Fifth Cavalry Monument. Courtesy of James Hatzell

Appendix

FIFTH CAVALRY COMMAND, JULY 17, 1876

Headquarters

- Colonel Wesley Merritt
- Lieutenant Colonel Eugene A. Carr
- Major John J. Upham
- First Lieutenant and Adjutant William C. Forbush
- Major Thaddeus H. Stanton, Paymaster
- Second Lieutenant J. Hayden Pardee, Twenty-third Infantry, Aide-de-camp
- Acting Assistant Surgeon Junius W. Powell
- Scout William F. Cody
- Scout Baptiste Garnier
- Scout Jonathan White
- Enlisted men on detail (four privates)
- Scouts (two mixed-bloods)

Total: 16

Company A

- Second Lieutenant Robert London*

Aggregate strength 47

Company B

- Captain Robert H. Montgomery

Aggregate strength 52

Company D

- Captain Samuel S. Sumner

Aggregate strength 55

Company G

- Captain Edward M. Hayes
- Second Lieutenant Hoel S. Bishop

Aggregate strength 47

Company I

- Captain Sanford C. Kellogg
- First Lieutenant Bernard Reilly, Jr.

Aggregate strength 46

Company K

- Major Julius W. Mason, Third Cavalry
- First Lieutenant Charles King

Aggregate strength 49

Company M

- Captain Edward H. Lieb

Aggregate strength 39

Total Fifth Cavalry Command in Warbonnet Creek Skirmish: 351

* London was detached from Company I. He had earlier been on detached service with Company D.

NOTES

[1] For overviews of the Great Sioux War, see Paul L. Hedren, "Introduction," *The Great Sioux War, 1876–77: The Best from Montana The Magazine of Western History* (Helena: Montana Historical Society 1991), 1–21; and Charles M. Robinson III, *A Good Year to Die, The Story of the Great Sioux War* (New York: Random House, 1995). For examinations of the war's southern front, see Paul L. Hedren, *Fort Laramie in 1876: Chronicle of a Frontier Post at War* (Lincoln: University of Nebraska Press, 1988); and Thomas R. Buecker, *Fort Robinson and the American West, 1874–1899* (Lincoln: Nebraska State Historical Society, 1999), chap. 3–5.

[2] Detailed for service were the headquarters detachment (Fort Hays), and companies A (Fort Hays), B (Fort Hays), C (Camp Supply, Indian Territory), D (Fort Hays), G (Camp Supply), I (Fort Gibson, Indian Territory), K (Fort Riley), and M (Fort Lyon, Colorado). George F. Price, *Across the Continent with the Fifth Cavalry* (New York: Antiquarian Press Ltd., 1959), 157; Charles King, *Campaigning With Crook and Stories of Army Life* (New York: Harper and Brothers, 1890), 3–9; Theo. F. Rodenbough and William L. Haskin, *The Army of the United States, Historical Sketches of Staff and Line with Portraits of Generals-in-Chief* (New York: Argonaut Press Ltd., 1966), 228–29.

[3] Fort Laramie Letters Sent, June 18, 1876, Record Group 393, Records of U.S. Army Continental Commands, National Archives and Records Administration, Washington, D. C. (hereafter cited as RG393). Copies of all Fort Laramie records cited in this history are located in the Fort Laramie National Historic Site Collections.

[4] James T. King, *War Eagle: A Life of General Eugene A. Carr* (Lincoln: University of Nebraska Press, 1963), 155.

[5] Hedren, *Fort Laramie in 1876*, 118; Don E. Alberts, *Brandy Station to Manila Bay, A Biography of General Wesley Merritt* (Austin, Tex.: Presidial Press, 1980), 227.

[6] Fort Laramie Endorsements, Endorsement on Orders No. 1, District of the Black Hills, June 19, 1876, RG393. Charles King's writings on the affair include *Campaigning With Crook*; "Long Distance Riding," *Cosmopolitan Magazine* (January 1894): 295–99; with Don Russell, "My Friend, Buffalo Bill," *The Cavalry Journal* 41 (September–October 1932): 17–20; "The Story of a March," *Journal of the United States Cavalry Association* 3 (June 1890): 121–29; "Details of Colonel Merritt's Charge on the Cheyennes," *New York Herald*, July 23, 1876; and "The War Bonnet," in *Indian Campaigns, Sketches of Cavalry Service in Arizona and on the Northern Plains by Captain Charles King*, ed. Harry H. Anderson (Fort Collins, Colo.: Old Army Press, 1984), 49–56.

[7] William A. Dobak, "Yellow Leg Journalists: Enlisted Men as Newspaper Reporters in the Sioux Campaign, 1876," *Journal of the West* 13 (January 1974): 97–98.

[8] Don Russell, "Cody, 'Buffalo Bill' [William Frederick]," in *The New Encyclopedia of the*

American West, ed. Howard R. Lamar (New Haven, Conn.: Yale University Press, 1998), 228–29. Among dozens of Cody biographies, the most reliable remains Don Russell's, *The Lives and Legends of Buffalo Bill* (Norman: University of Oklahoma Press, 1960).

[9] Cynthia J. Capron, "The Indian Border War of 1876," *Journal of the Illinois State Historical Society* 13 (January 1921): 488.

[10] Fort Laramie Endorsement No. 294, June 21, 1876, RG393; King, *Campaigning With Crook*, 113–14; Russell, *Lives and Legends*, 209–10.

[11] Russell, *Lives and Legends*, 220.

[12] James T. King, *War Eagle*, 155–56.

[13] Fort Laramie Medical History, entry dated June 14, 1876, RG393.

[14] Dobak, "Yellow Leg Journalists," 98–99. The bridge Powers refers to is a three-span truss constructed by the army in 1875, still standing today and carefully preserved within the bounds of Fort Laramie National Historic Site. The government ranch was a vegetable farm operated by Fort Laramie soldiers. Rawhide Station was a Cheyenne-Black Hills roadhouse.

[15] James T. King, *War Eagle*, 157.

[16] "C's" captain, Emil Adams, was attending district court in Dodge City, Kansas, and did not assume control of his company until July 7. Fifth Cavalry Muster Rolls, June-August, 1876, Record Group 94, Records of the Office of the Adjutant General, National Archives and Records Administration, Washington, D. C (hereafter cited as RG94); King, *Campaigning With Crook*, 9–10

[17] King, *Campaigning With Crook*, 16.

[18] King, "The Story of a March," 123.

[19] Fort Laramie Letters Sent, June 26, 1876, RG393.

[20] Fort Laramie Endorsements, Nos. 296/298, June 26, 1876, RG393.

[21] James T. King, *War Eagle*, 158.

[22] Ibid., 159.

[23] Price, *Across the Continent with the Fifth Cavalry*, 223–28; Paul Andrew Hutton, *Phil Sheridan and His Army* (Lincoln: University of Nebraska Press, 1985), 314–15; Alberts, *Brandy Station to Manila Bay*, 225–26.

[24] Price, *Across the Continent with the Fifth Cavalry*, 370–74. Mason officially joined his new regiment on Oct. 24, 1876.

[25] Alberts, *Brandy Station to Manila Bay*, 227–28; Fort Laramie Post Return, July 1876, RG393; King, *Campaigning With Crook*, 20.

[26] King, *Campaigning With Crook*, 20–22; Dobak, "Yellow Leg Journalists," 99; Price, *Across the Continent with the Fifth Cavalry*, 158.

[27] King, *Campaigning With Crook*, 23.

[28] Paul L. Hedren, ed., "Campaigning with the 5th Cavalry: Private James B. Frew's Diary and Letters from the Great Sioux War of 1876," *Nebraska History* 65 (Winter 1984): 449; Hedren, *Fort Laramie in 1876*, 107–8; Paul L. Hedren, "An Infantry Company in the Sioux Campaign, 1876," *Montana The Magazine of Western History* 33 (Winter 1983): 30–39.

[29] Fort Laramie Letters Sent, July 5, 1876, RG393.

[30] Ibid., July 6, 1876.

[31] Military Division of the Missouri Telegrams, July 6, 1876, RG393.

[32] Harry H. Anderson, "Charles King's Campaigning with Crook," *The Westerners (Chicago) Brand Book* 32 (January 1976): 66. "Mr. Lo," the term used by King in his letter, was a common frontier epithet originating in Alexander Pope's *Essay on Man*, one line of which read: "Lo, the poor Indian! whose untutored mind . . . ."

[33] Hedren, "Campaigning with the 5th Cavalry," 449.

[34] King, "Long Distance Riding," 297. For a penetrating analysis of Crook's dilemma and actions, see James T. King, "General Crook at Camp Cloud Peak: 'I Am at a Loss What to Do'" *Journal of the West* 9 (January 1972): 114–27.

[35] King, *Campaigning With Crook*, 24; Hedren, "Campaigning with the 5th Cavalry," 449; Dobak, "Yellow Leg Journalists," 99–100.

[36] The full details of Wilson's ploy were learned several years later when he attempted to have his commission restored. "In July, 1876, Wilson had tried to secure sick leave by swal-

lowing blood from a self-induced nose bleed and then spitting it up to represent hemorrhaging of the lungs. The surgeons detected the deception, and Wilson's resignation was submitted as an alternative to facing charges of malingering." Anderson, "Charles King's Campaigning With Crook," 67, 70.

[37] Fifth Cavalry, Company A Muster Roll, RG94.

[38] Fort Laramie Letters Sent, July 12, 1876, RG393; King, *Campaigning With Crook*, 25.

[39] Fifth Cavalry Regimental Return, July 1876, RG94. King, *Campaigning With Crook*, 25–26.

[40] Stanton Letter, Don Russell Papers, McCracken Research Library, Buffalo Bill Historical Center, Cody, Wyoming. The Carr and Little Wound references pertain to combat in the 1869 Republican River campaign. James T. King, *War Eagle*, chap. 5.

[41] Buecker, *Fort Robinson and the American West*, 81–82.

[42] Fort Laramie Letters Received, July 14, 1876, RG393. The Sitting Bull referred to was not the Hunkpapa medicine man prominent at the Little Big Horn and elsewhere, but an Oglala headman heretofore renowned for his friendliness toward the whites.

[43] King, *Campaigning With Crook*, 26-27.

[44] Letters Received by the Office of the Adjutant General, July 15, 1876 (Microcopy 666, Roll 271), RG94.

[45] King, *Campaigning With Crook*, 27.

[46] Ibid., 27–28, 33; Hedren, "An Infantry Company in the Sioux Campaign, 1876," 38; Dobak, "Yellow Leg Journalists," 100; Leander Richardson, "A Trip to the Black Hills," *Scribner's Monthly* 13 (April 1877): 750.

[47] King, "Long Distance Riding," 209.

[48] Ibid.

[49] King, *Campaigning With Crook*, 29–30.

[50] Charles King to Adelaide King, July 18, 1876, in Anderson, ed., *Indian Campaigns*, 99–100.

[51] Ibid.

[52] King, *Campaigning With Crook*, 32; James Willert, *After Little Bighorn, 1876 Campaign Rosters* (LaMirada, Calif.: James Willert, Publisher, 1985), 64.

[53] E. A. Brininstool, "Who Killed Yellow Hand?" *Outdoor Life Magazine* (February 1930): 12–13. These Cheyennes are occasionally reported to be followers of Little Wolf, and a few, in fact, were. In the main, however, these tribesmen were followers of Morning Star, who had not yet departed Red Cloud Agency for the Powder River Country. By this time, Little Wolf and most of his followers had allied with the northern Indians. Little Wolf himself joined the Little Big Horn River camp on the evening of June 25, the day of Custer's death. See Richard G. Hardorff, *Cheyenne Memories of the Custer Fight, A Source Book* (Spokane, Wash.: Arthur H. Clark Company, 1995), 86, 144, 152; John S. Gray, *Centennial Campaign, The Sioux War of 1876* (Fort Collins, Colo.: Old Army Press, 1976), 349; W. A. Graham, *The Custer Myth, A Source Book of Custeriana* (New York: Bonanza Books, 1953), 106, 114, 292.

[54] Don Russell, "The Duel on the Warbonnet," *The Journal of the American Military History Foundation* 1 (Summer 1937): 60; Chris Madsen, "Chris Madsen Finds the Spot," *Winners of the West*, Nov. 30, 1934.

[55] King, *Campaigning With Crook*, 36.

[56] "Statement of Sergeant John Hamilton, Troop D, Fifth Cavalry, to Brigadier General W. C. Brown, September 11, 1929," MS 6, William F. Cody Collection, Series IV, Johnny Baker Collection, McCracken Research Library, Buffalo Bill Historical Center, Cody, Wyoming.

[57] King, *Campaigning With Crook*, 42.

[58] Russell, *Lives and Legends*, 224.

[59] King and Russell, "My Friend, Buffalo Bill," 18; King, *Campaigning With Crook*, 36, 46. The other named soldiers were Second Lieutenant J. Hayden Pardee, Company H, Twenty-third Infantry, detached at Camp on Sage Creek when the Fifth Cavalry passed through on July 16 and now serving as an aide-de-camp to Merritt; and Sergeant Edmund Schreiber, Company K, Fifth Cavalry. Willert, *After Little Bighorn*, 64.

[60] King, *Campaigning With Crook*, 37.

[61] William F. Cody, *The Life of Hon. William F.*

Cody, Known as Buffalo Bill, The Famous Hunter, Scout and Guide (Hartford, Conn.: Frank E. Bliss, 1879; rpt., New York: Indian Head Books, 1991), 343–44.

[62] Ibid.; Christian Madsen Deposition, Aug. 28, 1929, Cody/Baker Collection; Statement of Sergeant John Hamilton.

[63] Cody, *The Life of Hon. William F. Cody*, 343–44; King, *Campaigning With Crook*, 37–38; Dobak, "Yellow Leg Journalists, 100. See also Russell, *Lives and Legends*, 230–35; and Russell, *Campaigning With King: Charles King, Chronicler of The Old Army* (Lincoln: University of Nebraska Press, 1991), 66–68, 161–63.

[64] Dobak, "Yellow Leg Journalists," 100; King, *Campaigning With Crook*, 38.

[65] King, *Campaigning With Crook*, 39.

[66] Ibid.; Dobak, "Yellow Leg Journalists," 100.

[67] Dobak, "Yellow Leg Journalists, 100.

[68] Regarding others who claimed to have slain Yellow Hair, see the following by Don Russell: *The Lives and Legends of Buffalo Bill*, 226–35; "Captain Charles King," *The Westerners New York Posse Brand Book* 4 (No. 2, 1957): 39–40; and "The Duel on the Warbonnet," 63–68. Regarding a motive for scalping Yellow Hair, see Paul L. Hedren, "The Contradictory Legacies of Buffalo Bill Cody's First Scalp for Custer," *Montana The Magazine of Western History* 55 (Spring 2005): 16–20. Regarding the scalping phenomenon, see Stanley Vestal, "The Duel With Yellow Hand," *Southwest Review* 26 (Autumn 1940): 76.

[69] Statement of Sergeant John Hamilton. Hamilton named the private with him "Daddy Aaron." Muster Rolls for Company D show no "Aaron" enlisted at the time, but confirm a Private Christian Ahrens. Willert, *After Little Bighorn*, 59.

[70] Brininstool, "Who Killed Yellow Hand?" 12.

[71] Dobak, "Yellow Leg Journalists." 100; Willert, *After Little Bighorn*, 59.

[72] King, *Campaigning With Crook*, 40-41.

[73] Military Division of the Missouri Telegrams, July 19 1876, RG393.

[74] James T. King, *War Eagle*, 162.

[75] Yellow Hair's name was mistakenly translated as Yellow Hand, and that name, in turn, consistently repeated by Cody and King and, thus, by most everyone else. But the correct name is assuredly Yellow Hair. See the statement given by his full sister, Josie Tangle-yellowhair, in Jerome A. Greene, ed., *Lakota and Cheyenne: Indian Views of the Great Sioux War, 1876–1877* (Norman: University of Oklahoma Press, 1994), 83. As to the corruption of the name, see Russell, *Lives and Legends*, 215.

[76] "Buffalo Bill Yarn is Verified Here," *Winners of the West*, Jan. 30, 1937; Russell, *Lives and Legends*, 230. The original letter is preserved today at the Buffalo Bill Historical Center, Cody, Wyoming.

[77] Cody, *The Life of Hon. William F. Cody*, 347; "Buffalo Bill Yarn is Verified Here"; Hedren, "The Contradictory Legacies of Buffalo Bill Cody's First Scalp for Custer," 20–22.

[78] "Details of Colonel Merritt's Charge on the Cheyennes," *New York Herald*, July 23, 1876, 7.

[79] The Powder River battle is ably chronicled by Jerome A. Greene in *Morning Star Dawn: The Powder River Expedition and the Northern Cheyennes, 1876* (Norman: University of Oklahoma Press, 2003). The magnitude of material culture loss is noted by Peter J. Powell, *Sweet Medicine: The Continuing Role of the Sacred Arrows, the Sun Dance, and the Sacred Buffalo Hat in Northern Cheyenne History*, vol. 1 (Norman: University of Oklahoma Press, 1969), 166–67.

[80] The phrase "Rule of 1876" referring to the surrender of persons, weapons, and horses appears in a communication between Brigadier General Alfred Terry and the Division of the Missouri, Mar. 24, 1881, in "Sioux Campaign," Special Files of Headquarters, Military Division of the Missouri, (Microcopy 1495, roll 5), RG393; Greene, *Morning Star Dawn*, 190–91; Buecker, *Fort Robinson and the American West*, 93–94.

[81] *New York Herald*, July 23, 1876; *Milwaukee Sentinel*, Nov. 8, 1879–Mar. 14, 1880; *Campaigning With Crook: The Fifth Cavalry in the Sioux War of 1876* (Milwaukee: Sentinel Company, 1880); King, *Campaigning With Crook*. See also Anderson, "Charles King's Campaigning With Crook,"65–67; and Russell, *Campaigning With King*, 64–68, 162.

[82] On King, see also Paul L. Hedren. "Charles King," in *Soldiers West: Biographies from the Military Frontier*, ed. Paul Andrew Hutton (Lincoln: University of Nebraska Press, 1987), 243–61; and Paul L. Hedren, "Introduction," in Russell, *Campaigning With King*, xv-xxiv. As well, see Harry H. Anderson, "The Friendship of Buffalo Bill and Charles King," *Milwaukee History: The Journal of the Milwaukee County Historical Society* 9 (Winter 1986): 119–32.

[83] Hedren, "The Contradictory Legacies of Buffalo Bill Cody's First Scalp for Custer," 16–35.

[84] History suggests that the main stem of this watercourse was known by the Oglala Sioux as Warbonnet Creek. As early as 1875, however, army officers mapped it as Hat Creek, likely an Americanization of Warbonnet. In Charles King's 1876 dispatch, he used both names, and did so again in his later writings. Merritt used Indian Creek in his report and so did others of the Fifth Cavalry. In reflecting on the fight in 1929, Beaver Heart, one of Yellow Hair's close companions, plainly declared that the episode occurred on Warbonnet Creek. Today Hat Creek generally prevails, and the name Warbonnet is reserved for a small tributary nearby.

[85] David Anderson, "'Fort' Montrose, Sioux County," *Nebraska History* 15 (April–June 1934): 114.

[86] Ibid., 114–15.

[87] J. B. Griffith, "The Story of How 'Buffalo Bill' Cody Killed Yellow Hand in a Hand-to-Hand Fight," ms., Wyoming State Archives and Historical Department, Cheyenne, Wyoming.

[88] Ibid.

[89] Charles King to Don Russell, Oct. 22, 1929, Don Russell Papers; Griffith, "The Story of How 'Buffalo Bill' Cody Killed Yellow Hand"; "Denver Veterans Will Help Locate Site of Indian Battle," undated newspaper clipping, William Carey Brown Papers, Western History Collections, University of Colorado Library, Boulder, Colorado.

[90] Griffith, "The Story of How 'Buffalo Bill' Cody Killed Yellow Hand"; "Chris Madsen Finds the Spot!"

[91] "Dedication Held in Sioux County," *Northwest Nebraska News*, Sept. 6, 1934; "Historic Monuments at Montrose," *Nebraska History* 15 (April–June 1934): 119–21; Hedren, "Introduction," *Campaigning with King*, by Don Russell, xix. Company D's captain, Samuel S. Sumner, lived until July 26, 1937. For an interesting footnote on Sumner, see Robert H. Davis, *On Home Soil with Bob Davis* (New York: D. Appleton and Company, 1930), 243–46.

[92] Henry J. Cordes, "Skirmish Site Monument Restored," *Omaha World-Herald*, May 17, 1999.

Bibliography

Manuscripts and Government Records

Brown, William Carey. Papers. Western History Collections, University of Colorado Library, Boulder, Colorado

Cody, William F. Collection. McCracken Research Library, Buffalo Bill Historical Center, Cody, Wyoming

Griffith, J. B. Manuscript. Manuscripts Division, Wyoming State Archives and Historical Department, Cheyenne, Wyoming.

Record Group 94, Records of the Office of the Adjutant General. AGO Letters Received 1876 (Microcopy 666, Roll 271); Fifth Cavalry Regimental Returns 1876; Fifth Cavalry Muster Rolls 1876. National Archives and Records Administration, Washington, D.C.

Record Group 393, Records of U. S. Army Continental Commands. Fort Laramie Endorsements 1876, Letters Received 1876, Letters Sent 1876, Medical History 1876, Post Returns 1876; Military Division of the Missouri Telegrams 1876, Special Files of Headquarters (Microcopy 1495, Roll 5). National Archives and Records Administration, Washington, D.C.

Russell, Don. Papers. McCracken Research Library, Buffalo Bill Historical Center, Cody, Wyoming.

Newspapers

Cheyenne Daily Leader

Milwaukee Sentinel

New York Herald

Crawford, Nebr., Northwest Nebraska News

Omaha World-Herald

Winners of the West

Books and Periodicals

Alberts, Don E. *Brandy Station to Manila Bay, A Biography of General Wesley Merritt* Austin, Tex.: Presidial Press, 1980.

Anderson, David. "'Fort' Montrose, Sioux County." *Nebraska History* 15 (April–June 1934): 114–15.

Anderson, Harry H. "Cheyennes at the Little Big Horn—A Study of Statistics." *North Dakota History* 27 (Spring 1960): 3–15.

__________. "Some Footnotes to Charles King's 'Campaigning With Crook.'" *Historical Messenger of the Milwaukee County Historical Society* 29 (Spring 1973): 2–25.

__________. "Charles King's Campaigning With Crook." *The Westerners (Chicago) Brand Book* 32 (January 1976): 65–67, 70–72.

__________. "The Friendship of Buffalo Bill and Charles King." *Milwaukee History: The Journal of the Milwaukee County Historical Society* 9 (Winter 1986): 119–32.

__________, ed. *Indian Campaigns, Sketches of Cavalry Service in Arizona and on the Northern Plains, by Captain Charles King*. Fort

Collins, Colo.: Old Army Press, 1984.

Brininstool, E. A. "Who Killed Yellow Hand?" *Outdoor Life Magazine* (February 1930): 12–13, 75–76.

Buecker, Thomas R. *Fort Robinson and the American West, 1874–1899*. Lincoln: Nebraska State Historical Society, 1999.

Capron, Cynthia J. "The Indian Border War of 1876." *Journal of the Illinois State Historical Society* 13 (January 1921): 476–503.

Cody, William F. *The Life of Hon. William F. Cody, Known as Buffalo Bill, The Famous Hunter, Scout and Guide*. Hartford, Conn.: Frank E. Bliss, 1879; rpt, New York: Indian Head Books, 1991.

_________. "My Duel With Yellow Hand." *Harper's Round Table* (September 1899): 521–25.

Davis, Robert H. *On Home Soil With Bob Davis*. New York: D. Appleton and Company, 1930.

Dobak, William A. "Yellow Leg Journalists: Enlisted Men as Newspaper Reporters in the Sioux Campaign, 1876." *Journal of the West* 13 (January 1974): 86–112.

Graham, W. A. *The Custer Myth, A Source Book of Custeriana*. New York: Bonanza Books, 1953.

Gray, John S. *Centennial Campaign: The Sioux War of 1876*. Fort Collins, Colo.: Old Army Press, 1976.

Greene, Jerome A., ed. *Lakota and Cheyenne: Indian Views of the Great Sioux War, 1876–1877*. Norman: University of Oklahoma Press, 1994.

_________. *Morning Star Dawn: The Powder River Expedition and the Northern Cheyennes, 1876*. Norman: University of Oklahoma Press, 2003.

Hardorff, Richard G., ed. *Cheyenne Memories of the Custer Fight, A Source Book*. Spokane, Wash.: Arthur H. Clark Company, 1995.

Hedren, Paul L. "An Infantry Company in the Sioux Campaign, 1876." *Montana The Magazine of Western History* 33 (Winter 1983): 30–39.

_________. "Campaigning with the 5th Cavalry: Private James B. Frew's Diary and Letters from the Great Sioux War of 1876." *Nebraska History* 65 (Winter 1984): 442–66.

_________. "Charles King." In *Soldiers West: Biographies from the Military Frontier*. Ed. Paul Andrew Hutton. Lincoln: University of Nebraska Press, 1987.

_________. *Fort Laramie in 1876: Chronicle of a Frontier Post at War*. Lincoln: University of Nebraska Press, 1988.

_________, ed. *The Great Sioux War, 1876–77: The Best from Montana The Magazine of Western History*. Helena: Montana Historical Society, 1991.

_________. "The Contradictory Legacies of Buffalo Bill Cody's First Scalp for Custer." *Montana The Magazine of Western History* 55 (Spring 2005): 16–35.

"Historic Monuments at Montrose." *Nebraska History* 15 (April–June 1934): 119–21.

Hutton, Paul Andrew, *Phil Sheridan and His Army*. Lincoln: University of Nebraska Press, 1985.

King, Charles. *Campaigning With Crook: The Fifth Cavalry in the Sioux War of 1876*. Milwaukee: Sentinel Company, 1880.

_________. *Campaigning With Crook and Stories of Army Life*. New York: Harper and Brothers, 1890.

_________. "The Story of a March." *Journal of the United States Cavalry Association* 3 (June 1890): 121–29.

_________. "Long Distance Riding." *Cosmopolitan Magazine* (January 1894): 295–302.

_________ and Don Russell. "My Friend, Buffalo Bill." *The Cavalry Journal* 41 (September–October 1932): 17–20.

King, James T. *War Eagle: A Life of General Eugene A. Carr*. Lincoln: University of Nebraska Press, 1963.

_________. "General Crook at Camp Cloud Peak: 'I Am at a Loss What to Do.'" *Journal of the West* 9 (January 1972): 114–27.

Powell, Peter J. *Sweet Medicine: The Continuing Role of the Sacred Arrows, the Sun Dance, and the Sacred Buffalo Hat in Northern Cheyenne History*. Vol. 1. Norman: University of Oklahoma Press, 1969.

Price, George F. *Across the Continent with the Fifth Cavalry*. New York: Antiquarian Press Ltd., 1959.

Richardson, Leander. "A Trip to the Black Hills." *Scribner's Monthly* 13 (April 1877): 748–56

Robinson, Charles M. III. *A Good Year to Die, The Story of the Great Sioux War*. New York: Random House, 1995.

Rodenbough, Theo. F., and William L. Haskin. *The Army of the United States, Historical Sketches of Staff and Line with Portraits of Generals-in-Chief*. New York: Argonaut Press Ltd., 1966.

Russell, Don. "The Duel on the Warbonnet." *The Journal of the American Military History Foundation* 1 (Summer 1937): 55–69.

_________. "Captain Charles King." *The Westerners New York Posse Brand Book* 4 (No. 2, 1957): 39–40.

_________. *The Lives and Legends of Buffalo Bill*. Norman: University of Oklahoma Press, 1960.

_________. "Cody, 'Buffalo Bill' [William Frederick]." In *The New Encyclopedia of the American West*. Ed. Howard R. Lamar. New Haven, Conn.: Yale University Press, 1998.

_________. *Campaigning With King: Charles King, Chronicler of the Old Army*. Lincoln: University of Nebraska Press, 1991.

Vestal, Stanley. "The Duel With Yellow Hand." *Southwest Review* 26 (Autumn 1940): 65–77.

Willert, James. *After Little Bighorn, 1876 Campaign Rosters*. LaMirada, Calif.: James Willert, Publisher. 1985.

Index

S

T

U

W

Y